WRITTEN SKILLS FOR

QUESTIONS & ANSWERS IN

DISPUTE RESOLUTION

Linda Chadderton and David Sixsmith

Series editors: Amy and David Sixsmith

REVISE
SQE

First published in 2024 by Fink Publishing Ltd

Impression number 10 9 8 7 6 5 4

British Library Cataloguing in Publication Data
A catalogue record for this book is available from the British Library
ISBN: 9781914213922

This book is also available in various ebook formats.
Ebook ISBN: 9781914213939

Cover and text design by BMLD (bmld.uk)
Production and typesetting by Westchester Publishing Services UK
Development editing by Llinos Edwards

Fink Publishing Ltd
E-mail: hello@revise4law.co.uk
www.revise4law.co.uk

Acknowledgements

Extracts from the SRA website in this book are owned by and published under licence from the Solicitors Regulation Authority of The Cube, 199 Wharfside Street, Birmingham, B1 1RN, which asserts its right to be identified as the author of this work in accordance with the Copyright, Designs and Patents Act 1988 Sections 77 and 78: www.sra.org.uk/solicitors/standards-regulations/financial-services-conduct-business-rules/. Please refer to the SRA website to ensure you are relying upon the correct version and most up to date version of the Standards.
Every effort has been made to obtain necessary permission with reference to copyright material. The publishers apologise if inadvertently any sources remain unacknowledged and will gladly make suitable arrangements with any copyright holders whom it has not been possible to contact.

Notes from the publisher

1. While Fink Publishing has made every attempt to ensure that advice on the qualification and its assessment is accurate, the official specification and associated assessment guidance materials are the only authoritative source of information and should always be referred to for definitive guidance. See the SRA website at https://sqe.sra.org.uk. Note that the SRA may amend their assessment guidance (including the contents of the assessment specifications) at any point.
2. Fink Publishing has robust editorial processes to ensure the accuracy of the content in this publication, and every effort is made to ensure this publication is free of errors. We are, however, only human, and occasionally errors do occur. Fink Publishing is not liable for any misunderstandings that arise as a result of errors in this publication, but it is our priority to ensure that the content is accurate. If you spot an error, please do contact us at **revise4law.co.uk** so we can make sure it is corrected.

Contents

Contributors

THE AUTHORS

Linda Chadderton is the Director of Professional Legal Education at the University of Lancashire, responsible for overseeing the professional graduate and postgraduate courses relating to law, having taught these courses for seven years. Linda is the author of *Revise SQE: Tort Law* and contributed to *Revise SQE: FLK1 Practice Assessment*. Linda is a solicitor and a fellow of Advance HE. Prior to entering academia she specialised in litigation working as a claimant solicitor initially for four years and then specialised in defendant litigation for 16 years thereafter. Linda has taught contract law and tort law to undergraduates and civil and criminal litigation, personal injury and clinical negligence, dispute resolution and professional conduct and ethics to postgraduate students. She also teaches SQE content on the Solicitor Degree Apprenticeship course.

Dr David Sixsmith is an assistant professor in law at Northumbria University, Newcastle. Previously a partner at a high-street law firm, he is now a non-practising solicitor and a senior fellow of Advance HE. His research specialism is in civil dispute resolution, and he teaches wills and administration of estates as well as trusts, at both undergraduate and postgraduate level. David is the author of *Revise SQE: Dispute Resolution*.

SERIES EDITORS

Dr Amy Sixsmith is associate professor in law at the University of Sunderland and a senior fellow of Advance HE.

Dr David Sixsmith is also an editor for this series.

Introduction

Welcome to *Revise SQE: Legal Skills for SQE2*! This series of revision guides is designed to guide you through the second element of your Solicitors Qualifying Examination, in which you will be tested on your ability to put the legal knowledge you acquired for your SQE1 assessment into six different practical contexts.

The key to successfully navigating your SQE2 assessment can be split into three distinct areas:
- understanding how you are being assessed and what you are being assessed on
- practising example scenarios
- comparing and contrasting your answers with sample answers.

Our SQE2 guides are here to help you with this process, providing you not only with helpful guidance and top tips for approaching all of the relevant skills, but also with multiple sample questions for each assessable skill in each of the relevant legal disciplines. Samples of high and lower scoring threshold answers to each question are provided, to guide you in good practice and steer you away from potential pitfalls.

Using this series in conjunction with our series of SQE1 revision guides, to ensure that your legal knowledge is accurate and up to date, will enable you to tackle your SQE2 assessment with confidence.

PREPARING YOURSELF FOR SQE

The SQE is the route to qualification for aspiring solicitors and consists of two parts, as shown in this table.

Assessment	Contents of assessment
SQE1	• 360 multiple-choice questions • Closed book • Assessed by two sittings • Over ten hours in total
SQE2	• Practical legal skills • 16 written and oral assessments • Assesses six practical legal skills • Over 14 hours in total

In addition to the above assessments, all candidates will have to undertake two years' qualifying work experience. More information on the SQE assessments can be found on the SRA website.

It is important to note that the SQE can be perceived to be a 'harder' set of assessments than the Legal Practice Course (LPC). The reason for this, explained by the SRA, is that the LPC is designed to prepare candidates for 'day one' of their training contract; the SQE, on the other hand, is designed to prepare candidates for 'day one' of being a newly qualified solicitor. With that in mind, and a different style of assessments in place, it is understandable that you might feel nervous or wary of the SQE.

This revision guide series will focus on preparation for SQE2. The SQE2 assessment is challenging as it asks candidates to put into practice the knowledge that they acquired for SQE1. This style of assessment is likely to be different from what you will have experienced before. In this Introduction and revision guide series, we hope to alleviate some of those concerns, with guidance on preparing for the SQE assessment, tips on how to approach the skills-based assessments and detailed commentaries on sample answers to aid your revision.

WHAT DOES SQE2 ENTAIL?

SQE2 is split into two parts: oral and written. The table below shows the contexts in which these skills are assessed.

Part	Skills	Contexts
Oral	Client interview and attendance note / legal analysis (hereafter referred to as 'interviewing')	Property practice Wills and intestacy, probate administration and practice
	Advocacy	Dispute resolution Criminal litigation
Written	Case and matter analysis Legal research Legal writing Legal drafting	Criminal litigation Dispute resolution Property practice Wills and intestacy, probate administration and practice Business organisations, rules and procedures

Oral skills
You will sit four oral skills examinations in two half-days.

On day one you will be assessed in:
• advocacy in the context of dispute resolution
• interviewing in the context of property practice.

On day two you will be assessed in:
• advocacy in the context of criminal litigation
• interviewing in the context of wills and intestacy, probate administration and practice.

Written skills
For the written skills assessment, you will sit 12 examinations which will take place over three half-days. Every day you will be required to take an assessment in *each* of the written skills – legal research, case and matter analysis, legal writing and legal drafting.

On day one you will sit:
• two assessments in dispute resolution
• two assessments in criminal litigation.

On day two you will sit:
• two assessments in property practice
• two assessments in wills and intestacy, probate administration and practice.

On day three you will sit all four assessments in business organisations, rules and procedures.

HOW IS SQE2 MARKED?

Each of the SQE2 skills has its own set of assessment criteria. The *Revise SQE: Legal Skills for SQE2* series will include the following:

- Oral skills – the criteria are outlined in **Oral Skills for SQE2: Client Interviewing and Negotiation** and **Oral Skills for SQE2: Advocacy**.
- Written skills – the criteria are outlined at the beginning of each chapter in our books covering the written skills for different legal contexts (see pages 2, 21, 56 and 69 in this text).

The assessment is marked against the relevant criteria using the following scale:

A. Superior performance: well above the competency requirements of the assessment.
B. Clearly satisfactory: clearly meets the competency requirements of the assessment.
C. Marginal pass: on balance, just meets the competency requirements of the assessment.
D. Marginal fail: on balance, just fails to meet the competency requirements of the assessment.
E. Clearly unsatisfactory: clearly does not meet the competency requirements of the assessment.
F. Poor performance: well below the competency requirements of the assessment.

Your mark will be calculated by converting the grade into a numerical mark, with A representing 5 marks and F representing 0 marks.

The scaled scoring system

In January 2025 the SRA introduced a scaled scoring system for all SQE2 assessments. This approach is designed to ensure that candidate scores are comparable across different assessment sittings, thereby providing a fair and consistent measure of candidate performance. The same system has already been implemented for all SQE1 assessments.

The scaled scoring system works in the following way:

- Initially, candidates will receive a 'raw score' based on their performance across the 16 assessment stations in SQE2.
- A pass mark is then set for each assessment window. The pass mark is determined using statistical methods that account for any differences in question difficulty. This ensures fairness across different exam versions.
- Candidate raw scores are then converted to a common scale ranging from 0 to 500, with the pass mark consistently set at 300. This standardisation allows for direct comparisons between candidates' performances, regardless of the specific assessments they completed.

When you access your results, you will be able to see:

- a detailed breakdown of your results by assessment station (results will be expressed as marks from 0 to 5 for each assessment criterion across each of the 16 assessment stations)
- your overall mark expressed as a percentage
- your scaled score out of 500 – remember that the pass mark will always be set at 300.

For more information about the scaled scoring system, visit https://sqe.sra.org.uk/SQEHomePage.

It is very important that you are aware of the standard you are required to meet. The competence standard is that of a Day One Solicitor, which is mapped against Level 3 of the Threshold Standard for the Statement of Solicitor Competence. This is available on the SRA website, and we would encourage you to review this prior to sitting your SQE2 assessment.

The assessors

In terms of who will be assessing you against this standard, and the relevant skills criteria, the interview will be marked by the person you are interviewing, whilst the remaining assessments (attendance note, advocacy and all written skills) will be marked by a solicitor. All assessors will have received training on how to assess a candidate's performance against the relevant criteria. It is therefore essential that you tackle your assessments in the same way that you would if you were a fully qualified solicitor on the first day of practice – with professionalism, confidence and calmness. This will come across to the assessors in the examination itself: remember that they are fundamentally assessing your suitability for practice!

WHERE DOES *REVISE SQE* COME INTO IT?

This new series of revision guides for SQE2 will provide you with helpful tips and advice on how to tackle each skill assessment in the relevant contexts. Each book provides a range of example threshold answers to SQE2-style assessment questions, which you can use to practise and assess your answers against, to see how you are performing in each individual area. This is designed to assist with your revision and consolidate your understanding of how key topics could be assessed in the SQE2 examinations. We hope that this series will give clarity for the assessment focus, provide useful tips for sitting SQE2 and also act as a general revision aid.

Finally, always keep in mind that while SQE2 is primarily a skills-based assessment, you are still being tested on your knowledge of the law. It is therefore important that you conduct an honest self-evaluation on the areas of the SQE1 specification with which you feel you need further support. *Revise SQE* can help you with this:

- Check out the 'SQE1 Revision Checklist' for each of our SQE1 revision guides on our website: **www.revise4law.co.uk**. These will help you to identify which substantive topics you feel confident about being assessed on, and which ones you need to revise.
- All of our *Revise SQE* revision guides are mapped to the relevant SRA specifications for SQE1. Before taking the SQE2 assessments, remember to look back at our revision guides for SQE1 if you have any gaps in your legal knowledge.

1

Case and matter analysis

■ MAKE SURE YOU KNOW

This chapter deals with the skill of case and matter analysis in the context of dispute resolution. This is one of the legal skills that may be assessed in dispute resolution on day one of the SQE2 assessments (see the Introduction for more detail). You will be required to apply contractual or tortious principles to the processes associated with dispute resolution, so you will need a sound knowledge of these different areas of the law. We therefore advise you to revise the contents of *Revise SQE: Dispute Resolution*, *Revise SQE: Tort Law* and *Revise SQE: Contract Law* before attempting the questions in this chapter.

Some of the scenarios used in the practice examples contained in those books are built on below, to show you how the SQE2 skills assessment tests your knowledge of the legal principles you will have learned for your SQE1 examinations. This chapter provides examples of how different elements of contractual and tortious disputes can arise in the context of an SQE2 case and matter analysis assessment.

■ SQE ASSESSMENT ADVICE

As you work through this chapter, remember to pay particular attention in your revision to:
- identifying the relevant facts
- providing client-focused advice
- ensuring your advice demonstrates an understanding of the problem from the client's point of view and what the client wants to achieve, not just from a legal perspective
- using clear, precise, concise and acceptable language
- applying the law correctly to the client's situation
- applying the law comprehensively to the client's situation, identifying any ethical and professional conduct issues and exercising judgement to resolve them honestly and with integrity.

See the Appendix for the SRA's performance indicators in case and matter analysis.

■ INTRODUCTION TO CASE AND MATTER ANALYSIS IN DISPUTE RESOLUTION

The SQE2 assessment will probably replicate scenarios that occur in everyday legal practice. When practising in the field of dispute resolution, you need to develop the ability to consider the details of a case, analyse the facts to ascertain whether the matter can be resolved in the best interest of the client and then provide advice to the client.

The SQE2 assessment in case and matter analysis will be based on a case study with documents on which you will be asked to produce a written report to a partner, giving a legal analysis of the case and providing client-focused advice. This may or may not include options and strategies for negotiation. This chapter will provide examples of how you can do this whilst meeting the assessment criteria for SQE2 case and matter analysis.

To create a logical and clear response to your SQE2 case and matter analysis assessment, approach the question in a structured manner. Try adopting the following method:

1. Once you have read the case details and the documentation, write down the key facts and legal issues that are relevant to the matter.
2. You can then structure your written report around those key facts and legal issues by using headings or sub-headings.
3. Complete your written report.
4. Review your answer, keeping in mind the SQE2 case and matter analysis assessment criteria.

Assessment technique

When reviewing your answer, check you have dealt with each relevant fact or legal issue, cross-referencing the relevant information presented in the documents and case study. This prevents you from omitting important information.

SQE2 case and matter analysis assessment criteria

Try to remember these points as you construct your answer:

Skills

1. Identify relevant facts.
2. Provide client-focused advice (ie advice which demonstrates an understanding of the problem from the client's point of view and what the client wants to achieve, not just from a legal perspective).
3. Use clear, precise, concise and acceptable language.

Application of law

4. Apply the law correctly to the client's situation.
5. Apply the law comprehensively to the client's situation, identifying any ethical and professional conduct issues and exercising judgement to resolve them honestly and with integrity.

In chapter 2 of **Revise SQE: Contract Law**, we considered the performance of existing duties and consideration. Question 1 below demonstrates how your knowledge of this topic could be tested in the context and format of an SQE2 case and matter analysis assessment.

■ QUESTION 1

Email to candidate

From: Partner
Sent: 2 April 202#
To: Candidate
Subject: Amir Singh, Singh Electrical Ltd

Yesterday I spoke to a new client, Amir Singh. Amir is the director of Singh Electrical Ltd, which is a medium-sized local business providing electrical services to the local area. Amir explained that he started the business ten years ago and has gradually built up a good client base. He provides electrical services for some local companies and also long-standing clients in the community.

Amir admitted that he is not great with paperwork. Most of his clients are repeat business, and over the years he has come to various ad hoc agreements with them about the cost, supply and billing of his services. Most of his original agreements were verbal but he has started to draw contracts up for his new business clients. Amir feels that due to his kind nature and relaxed attitude to payment, some of his clients are taking advantage of him. Some clients have fallen behind on their payments to him while others have failed to pay for the services provided. His company is now suffering cash-flow problems as a result. I took details of the payment issues he is experiencing with two separate clients. They are as follows:

Saaima Iqbal

Saaima Iqbal runs a number of beauty salons in the town and intended to expand her business by opening a further three salons. Amir agreed to undertake all the electrical work for the new salons last year. They agreed that the work would be completed for all three salons in four weeks, as Saaima wanted to time the launch with a new advertising campaign she had committed to.

Unfortunately, some of Amir's employees contracted COVID-19, and being short-staffed he advised Saaima that he would be unable to complete the work to the original four-week deadline. Amir explained to me that Saaima was really disappointed and wanted him to prioritise her work. She offered Amir an extra 20% on the price she had agreed to pay if he completed the work to the original four-week deadline. Amir agreed and managed to complete the three salons on time. The original price agreed was £10,000 and Saaima had offered a further £2,000 if completed on time.

Saaima has only paid Amir £10,000. He wants to know whether he can pursue her for the extra £2,000. There was no written agreement, as Saaima is a friend of his wife's and he did not think about putting the verbal agreement or the offer of extra payment in writing at that stage. Amir is also rather concerned that he gave Saaima a low quote because she is a friend of his wife. On reflection, he explained that the work was really worth about £15,000.

Shakira Umbridge

Amir has recently agreed to undertake some work for Shakira Umbridge in their property. He rewired the house, and purchased and fitted new light fittings. His total bill came to £2,500. He was due to complete the work on 1 April and as with all his invoices, payment was due 14 days after completion of works.

Shakira is a self-employed joiner and was recently involved in a road traffic accident in which they suffered soft tissue injuries, which have prevented them from working for the last two months. Shakira spoke to Amir at the beginning of March before he had finished the work, telling him they were experiencing financial hardship and cash-flow issues. As a concession, Amir verbally agreed to reduce the bill to £1,250, but on condition that it was paid on the date of completion. Shakira paid £1,250 on 1 April when the work was completed. However, as Amir is now experiencing cash-flow problems, he wants to know whether he can go back to Shakira and ask for the residual amount. He explained that Shakira is now fully recovered and that they received compensation for their road traffic accident so are likely to be able to afford the remaining amount.

Advice and analysis required
Amir would like advice on how best to secure the amounts owed to his company. He does not want to damage his reputation but is under increasing pressure due to lack of cash flow caused by clients not paying his full bill.

Please provide advice and analysis for me to use as the basis of a letter to the client. In providing your advice, please bear in mind that Amir is not a lawyer but does have experience of running a business. The client would like brief explanations of the relevant law, where appropriate, so please include these in your advice and analysis. Do not include advice about the procedure at this stage as we have just been asked to provide an overview of Amir's legal position in respect of the outstanding amounts. There is also no need to explore promissory estoppel.

Please set out your advice and analysis on the following:

1. If Saaima Iqbal refuses to pay the extra 20% on the price, does Amir have any legal entitlement to require her to do so?
2. Can Amir pursue Shakira for the full amount now that they have received money from their compensation claim?

You do not need to consider any client-care matters.

Thanks,

Partner

* * *

■ YOUR TURN
Have a go at answering question 1, remembering the guidance on pages 1–2.
• Refer to the structured approach in the SRA's assessment criteria on page 2.
• Create a list of the most salient legal issues raised by the question.
• Timings are important: you will need to prepare and write your answer in one hour.

SQE1 Functioning legal knowledge link
Remember from chapter 3 of *Revise SQE: Contract Law* that the intention to create legal relations is one of the four key requirements to make a contract legally binding, and it is required for all contracts.

EVALUATING YOUR ANSWER

When you have attempted question 1, mark it yourself against the SQE2 case and matter analysis criteria. Do you think your attempt met the threshold standard?

Now compare your attempt with the following key legal points and two sample answers to the question. A circled number indicates that commentary is provided for this part of the answer. The commentary explains whether or not the sample satisfies the assessment criteria, and accordingly likely to meet the threshold SQE2 standard.

➡Key legal points: Question 1

- Contract: you will need to explain the requisite ingredients to form a legally binding contract. You will then need to consider whether an oral agreement can constitute a legally binding contract. In order to consider whether Amir and Saaima, and also Amir and Shakira, have a contract, you will need to consider whether there has been an offer, acceptance of the offer, consideration and certainty of terms, and whether both parties intended to enter legal relations.
- Consideration: you will then need to explain consideration – promise/act of value in exchange for an act/promise of value. Is the offer of money by Saaima to Amir in the first instance, in exchange for services, consideration? Have the parties given consideration for any of the arrangements? Is Saaima's offer to pay an extra 20% adequate or sufficient consideration? Remember that consideration must not be past.
- Consequences of a promise: the issues in respect of Amir and Saaima are the consequences of a promise to pay more for the performance of an existing contractual duty owed to a promisor; and in respect of Amir and Shakira, the consequences of a promise to pay less under an existing contract.

■ SAMPLE ANSWER 1 TO QUESTION 1

The requisite ingredients to form a legally binding contract are offer, acceptance, consideration and intention to create legal relations. A contract can be verbal or in writing. Amir has conceded that his business arrangements going forward will be evidenced in writing, which is appropriate. ❶

Offer and acceptance along with an intention to create legal relations are all evident in respect of both the work completed for Saaima Iqbal and Shakira Umbridge. Whether or not Amir can pursue either party for outstanding amounts will depend upon whether there was consideration. Consideration is generally a promise of an act or omission, or an act or omission in exchange for the same. Consideration does not need to be adequate but only sufficient, although it must not be past. The amount offered under the contract does not need to match the value of the work done. Also of note is the fact that the work was carried out after the contract was entered into. ❷

Saaima Iqbal ❸

Constituent parts of contract are evident – offer, acceptance and the intention to create legal relations. Turning to consideration, Amir did what he was already bound to do under the verbal agreement. He agreed with Saaima that the work would be complete within four weeks, due to Saaima's offer to increase payment by 20%. The general approach is that if parties to a contract agree that one party will pay more than was agreed under the original contract, the promise to pay more is not binding unless the promisee makes an additional promise, act or omission as consideration. Without this Amir is doing nothing more than he was contractually bound to do under the original agreement with Saaima. As long as Amir has not provided any additional consideration then he is unable to pursue Saaima for the 20% uplift on his bill. If Amir had, for example, employed more staff to get the job done on time then potentially he could pursue Saaima for the extra 20%, because a key element of consideration is 'exchange', and Amir would have provided something additional (ie more staff) for Saaima's additional offer of 20%. ❹

We must also consider the additional test of practical benefit. Did Saaima obtain a practical benefit as a result of making the promise to pay more? If she did, the practical benefit is the consideration itself, which makes the promise legally binding. We may be able to argue that the practical benefit for Saaima was the opening of her salons on time without having to delay publicity and marketing, etc. We could advise Amir that reimbursement of the 20% is likely to fail due to lack of consideration, but we could try to negotiate with Saaima on that basis. If she is a friend of his wife, she might wish to settle this amicably. ❺

The fact that Amir feels he had undervalued his work is of no consequence, as consideration only has to be sufficient not adequate. Amir agreed the figure of £10,000, and whether or not this is adequate has no effect on the contract as it was sufficient. ❻

If Saaima Iqbal refuses to pay the extra 20% on the price, Amir does not have any legal entitlement to require her to do so. ❼

Shakira Umbridge

Constituent parts of contract are evident – offer, acceptance and the intention to create legal relations. Turning to consideration, a promise to pay less than is owed under an existing contract is not consideration. However, an exception to that rule is that if the payment is required before the original amount was due. Amir reduced his bill to £1,250 and required it to be paid on 1 April instead of within 14 days of completion of the works: Shakira has therefore provided consideration, and as a result Amir is unable to pursue them for the outstanding amount. The fact that they received compensation due to an accident recently is not relevant. ❽

COMMENTARY

❶ The introductory paragraph sets out the relevant facts, and the purpose of the memorandum. It is important to clearly establish the relevant facts from the outset, and what the client is seeking advice on – the candidate then needs to maintain that client-focused approach throughout the memorandum. The candidate should remember to show the examiners that they can analyse a case and apply the law to the scenario to give a solution to the client. The analysis starts with an overview of the requirements of a legally binding contract, which should be a starting point for any discussion on whether the parties are bound by their subsequent additional agreements. It is important to note that the contract can be verbal or in writing, and that the client has been conducting his business without written agreements, although it is not advisable to do so.

❷ Moving on from dealing with the basics of a contract, the analysis discusses consideration, which is a constituent element when entering into a contract. The language is clear and will be easily understandable for the client.

❸ This section deals with aspects of the first contract with Saaima Iqbal. The candidate has remembered the SQE2 assessment criteria and set out their answer logically and clearly. Breaking the issues down in this way and using headings makes for better reading.

❹ Now that the basics have been explained, the analysis goes into further detail about whether Saaima is bound to pay the extra 20%, and what other elements need to be considered. Using an example is a good way of explaining a legal principle to a client.

Explaining the issues relating to the client and applying the principles here shows the examiner that the candidate not only understands the law but can apply it to the scenario.

5 The candidate should always be ready to argue a counterpoint or highlight weaknesses in the argument put forward on behalf of the client. They need to ensure the client's expectations are managed. Dealing with each issue/third party in turn presents a clear structure and ensures that the issues are explored in sufficient depth, applying relevant law and providing the client with a clear answer. Here the candidate considers that the client has a connection to the third party and this should be taken into consideration when attempting to negotiate the issue.

6 The law is again applied to the scenario, showing the assessor a firm grasp of the issues, which in turn provides clarity on the client's legal position.

7 The candidate should always provide an answer to the question posed. It is not sufficient to write about contract law. The assessors are judging the candidate on whether they can use the information supplied, apply the law and actually present the client with a solution or answer to the problem.

8 Reiterating the issues and dealing with them in a methodical manner ensures that all points are dealt with. It is important to manage the client's expectations regarding the third party's receipt of compensation, namely that this is of no consequence to the legal issues involved.

Does this answer meet the threshold?
The sample answer above contains all of the information that the client requires and that the candidate has been asked to provide. It is therefore likely to meet the threshold standard for the SQE2 case and matter analysis. Note how each of the assessment criteria for the case and matter analysis are dealt with, and where appropriate the assessor is directed specifically to the areas of the analysis, which deal with those criteria. It is important for the candidate to show that they are familiar with the criteria by which they are being assessed.

Now consider the second sample answer to question 1.

■ SAMPLE ANSWER 2 TO QUESTION 1

In order to consider the issues we need to establish that this is a contractual matter. In order to form a contract, there needs to be offer and acceptance. An offer is a willingness to enter into legal relations and is binding as soon as it is accepted. The offer is a statement and terms that the person making the offer – here Amir – is willing to enter into legal relations with the other party. An acceptance is either an act or a promise to be bound by the terms of the offer that has been made by Amir. **1**

The issue is whether Amir can force Saaima to pay him the extra 20% and whether he can force Shakira to pay him the £1,250 owed. **2**

Amir had agreed to pull out all the stops and get Saaima's salons up and running, and he was kind enough to reduce the bill for Shakira. He now wants to know whether he can sue them for the outstanding amounts. **3**

The issue here is whether there was consideration between any of the parties. When Amir agreed to put in extra work for Saaima, he provided consideration as he would have to get more staff or work longer hours. **4**

When he reduced Shakira's bill, he did so to maintain good will with clients. Now that Shakira has received more money, a claim against them is possible. We could write to them and point this out as a tactic, although because they paid before the due date they have acted, and a court may find that they have done what was expected of them. ❺

In conclusion, a threat to issue court proceedings against both Saaima and Shakira may force them to pay an amount to Amir. ❻

COMMENTARY

❶ The candidate has discussed only two elements that constitute a contract – offer and acceptance. They have omitted the other essential elements, namely an intention to create legal relations and consideration.

❷ Opening with the issues in question is advisable, but a further explanation of the legal issues should follow in order to enable proper analysis of the case. There is no application here of whether Amir and Shakira or Saaima have entered into binding contracts, and no discussion of whether the contracts would be affected by being verbal only.

❸ We do not know whether the client 'agreed to pull out all the stops'; this is just their perception of the situation. Do not make assumptions: if the client had confirmed this, an opinion could be formed. However, there is an intimation here that Amir has worked over and above that which was expected, which in the context of the issues could actually change the advice. Working over and above that expected or laying on extra staff would be deemed to be consideration, and accordingly Amir could pursue Saaima for the extra 20% promised. Note also that this paragraph just repeats the information provided in the partner's memo. As the assessment time limit is one hour, the candidate needs to use this time to address the issues, not repeat the question.

❹ The issues do relate to consideration, but there should be an explanation about what this entails. The partner is using the case and matter analysis to form the basis of their advice to the client. The terms should be explained, in appropriate language, to ensure the client understands the legal position. There is also a further assumption that the client has provided more staff – this is not confirmed and should not be assumed. Relevant facts only should be dealt with.

❺ The analysis is too brief. The conclusion is reached before proper consideration of all the relevant facts and legal issues. The candidate should go through each client's specific issues separately, and not group them together. Ultimately, in respect of both Saaima and Shakira there is not sufficient consideration, so the client's expectations need to be managed.

❻ Advising that legal proceedings are threatened is unethical at this stage. Notwithstanding it ignores the overriding objective of the Civil Procedure Rules (CPR), the candidate has failed to consider what effect this may have on Amir or his relationship with his wife and her friend, Saaima. There has also been a failure to identify the relevant legal issues regarding consideration, specifically whether early payment or the promise of extra payment would be regarded as due consideration. A more appropriate tactic might be to advise Amir that he could approach both clients and explain his situation, in the hope that they are sympathetic to his cash-flow problems. There is no specific protocol for contractual claims but the practice direction on pre-action protocols and conduct should be adhered to, which means that if Amir wishes to pursue the matter, a letter could be sent to both third parties in an attempt to notify them of the issue and potentially negotiate.

Does this answer meet the threshold?

When assessing the second case and matter analysis sample answer against the SQE2 case and matter analysis criteria, it is unlikely that this would meet the threshold standard for SQE2 case and matter analysis. The skills relevant to the threshold standard include identifying relevant facts, providing client-focused advice and using clear, precise, concise and acceptable language. To meet the threshold standard, the candidate should apply the law correctly and comprehensively to the client's situation, identifying any ethical and professional conduct issues and exercising judgement to resolve the issues honestly and with integrity. The second sample answer lacks correct information, fails to consider all the issues and makes assumptions.

SQE2 can assess any of the areas on the SQE1 dispute resolution specification. Below is another example of how a different part of the specification could arise in the context of SQE2 case and matter analysis.

■ QUESTION 2

Email to candidate

From: Partner
Sent: 9 February 202#
To: Candidate
Subject: Subha Kulendiren – Dispute with Tuckers Wood Ltd

Yesterday I spoke to a new client, Subha Kulendiren, about problems she has had with furniture produced by Tuckers Wood Designs (TWD). TWD is a company that produces and supplies wood sculptures. Subha owns a large, contemporary new-build house in a rural setting just outside Clitheroe. On completion of the garden room and landscaping, Subha wanted to install bespoke garden furniture created by TWD.

Subha undertook some online research and located TWD due to their large Instagram following. She contacted the owner Nathan Tucker, who advised that he specialised in one-off sculptural designs and could design any furniture Subha required.

Subha confirmed she visited TWD's workshop on 31 July 202# with her sister, Ansitha. She states she had a lengthy discussion with Nathan about the types of items she required. The client told Nathan about her recent house move and described the house's large garden room and extensive landscaped gardens. Subha said that she explained in some detail that she wanted all of the furniture to look like works of art. It was also important to her that the wood be sourced from the UK and from sustainable forests. She said that she wanted these pieces of furniture to stay at the property and be in the family for generations.

Subha mentioned that Nathan seemed to fully appreciate what she was saying, and he told her that his work would withstand the test of time. Subha wanted a table and six chairs, and also a statement bench, as a real feature. She was advised the cost was dependent upon the precise materials used but that the figure would be between £75,000 and £100,000. The client placed an order and was advised that it would take about four months to complete. Subha confirmed that Nathan noted the information on his phone and she paid a deposit of £5,000.

Subha took delivery of the furniture on 14 December 202#. The total cost was £79,500 and she paid the outstanding amount of £74,500 immediately. The product was delivered by Great Lancashire logistics and installed where the client indicated in her garden. Initially, the client was delighted with the furniture. She had specialist interior and exterior lighting fitted to illuminate the pieces and she held many parties to show it off.

However, the client advised that during cold weather in January, she noticed that cracks had appeared around some of the joints on the chairs, making them unsafe to sit on, and also that the surface of the wood was bubbling. It looked as if the finish on the wood was coming away. Subha contacted TWD and Nathan Tucker attended her property (Ansitha, Subha's sister was also present). Nathan was shocked when he examined the furniture as he maintained he had no idea that the wood was to be placed outside: he thought it was for use in the new garden room. Subha expressed her surprise at this as his company had installed them outside. Nathan advised that they outsource installation to Great Lancashire logistics. He told the client that the wood that he used, and the oil used as the finish, were only suitable for inside use. He also said that Subha had wanted sculptures that looked like pieces of furniture and so he was not aware that they were going to be used. He made pieces of art not furniture, and never envisaged anyone sitting on the chairs or bench.

Subha's friend, who is a structural engineer, knows a lot about wood. He inspected the furniture and says that it seems to be made of a European softwood, which would be completely unsuitable for outside. All wood has an OSM mark (origin and sustainability mark). He told her that the marks on the furniture clearly indicate that it has come from another European country and it is very unlikely to be from a sustainable forest. The way that the wood has been joined together is also completely unsuitable for any weight-bearing whatsoever.

The client is very upset. She has suffered disappointment and mental distress, and in her own words she wants to 'take him for every penny he's got'. She wants proceedings issued and the matter to proceed to court as quickly as possible. She has provided a copy of the signed contract (Attachment 1).

Advice and analysis required
Please provide advice and analysis for me to use as the basis of a letter to the client. In providing your advice, please bear in mind that the client is eager to issue proceedings; she would like a brief explanation of the relevant law, where appropriate, so please include this in your advice and analysis. Please DO NOT provide any advice regarding funding as the client has received a client-care letter dealing with this and has been advised about this issue separately.

Please set out your advice and analysis on the following:

1.   **What does the client need to prove to successfully recoup the investment in the furniture? You should include a brief explanation of the relevant law, any anticipated counter-arguments Tuckers Wood Ltd may raise and the remedies available to the client.**
2.   **Provide details of the process involved in pursuing Tuckers Wood Ltd in a legal action. Are there any factors which prevent the client bringing court proceedings immediately?**

Thanks,

Partner

Note to candidates:

Please assume that there is no conflict of interest. I have dealt with all client-care matters, so you do not need to consider these.

Attachment 1

We are Tuckers Wood Ltd, a company registered in England and Wales under company number: 696516

Our registered office is at: Tuckers Yard, Prestown, Greater Lancashire

Our VAT number is: 7896425

1 Introduction

1.1   If you buy goods and services from us you agree to be legally bound by this contract.
These terms and conditions apply only if you are buying goods and services from us as a consumer (ie for purposes outside of your business, craft or profession). If you are buying goods and services from us in the course of business, our business terms and conditions apply to such purchases. For a copy of such terms, please speak to us in store or visit the following website: www.tuckerssculptures.com.

1.2   When buying any goods and services from us you also agree to be legally bound by:

1.2.1   extra terms which may add to, or replace some of, this contract. We will contact you to let you know if we intend to do this by giving you one month's notice.

1.2.2   specific terms which apply to certain goods or services (or both). If you want to see these specific terms, please check against the relevant goods in store or speak with us in store about the services (or both).

All of the above documents form part of this contract as though set out in full here.

2 Information we give you

2.1   By law, the Consumer Contracts (Information, Cancellation and Additional Charges) Regulations 2013 say that we must give you certain key information before a legally binding contract between you and us is made (see the summary box below).

We will give you information on:
- the main characteristics of the goods and services you want to buy;
- who we are, where we are based and how you can contact us;
- the total price of the goods and services including any taxes (or where this cannot reasonably be worked out in advance, the manner in which we will work out the price);
- all additional delivery and installation charges (or where this cannot reasonably be worked out in advance, the fact that such additional charges may be payable);
- the arrangements for payment, delivery, installation, performance, and the time by which we will deliver and install the goods;
- the arrangements for payment, carrying out of the services, and the time by which we will carry out the services;
- our complaint handling policy;
- the fact that we are under a legal duty to supply goods that are in conformity with the contract;
- our after-sales services;
- our commercial guarantees; and
- how long the contract is for and how to end it.

2.2   We will give you this information in a clear and understandable way. Typically, we will do this in store before you buy the goods and services from us. Some of this information is likely to be obvious from the context. Some of this information is also set out in this contract, such as information on our complaint handling policy (see Clause 14).

2.3   The key information we give you by law forms part of this contract (as though it is set out in full here).

2.4   If we have to change any key information once a legally binding contract between you and us is made, we can only do this if you agree to it.

3 Your privacy and personal information

3.1   Our **Privacy Policy** is available at www.tuckerssculptures.com.

3.2   Your privacy and personal information are important to us. Any personal information that you provide to us will be dealt with in line with our Privacy Policy, which explains what personal information we collect from you, how and why we collect, store, use and share such information, your rights in relation to your personal information, and how to contact us and supervisory authorities if you have a query or complaint about the use of your personal information.

4 Ordering goods and services from us

4.1   Below, we set out how a legally binding contract between you and us is made.

4.2   Any quotation given by us before you make an order for goods and services is not a binding offer by us to supply such goods and services.

4.3   When you decide to place an order for goods and services with us, this is when you offer to buy such goods and services from us.

4.4   When you place your order with us, we will acknowledge it in store. This acknowledgement does not, however, mean that your order has been accepted by us.

4.5   We may contact you to say that we do not accept your order. This is typically for the following reasons:

4.5.1 we cannot carry out the services (for example, because we have a shortage of staff);

4.5.2 the goods are unavailable;

4.5.3 we cannot authorise your payment.

4.6   We will only accept your order when we email you to confirm this (**Confirmation Email**). At this point:

4.6.1 a legally binding contract will be in place between you and us;

4.6.2 we will start to carry out the services in the way you and we have agreed; and

4.6.3 we will dispatch the goods to you and install the goods.

4.7   If you are under the age of 18 you may OR may not buy any goods and services from us. You may not be able to buy certain goods or services (or both) because you are too young.

5 Delivery and installation of goods

If we need to deliver goods to you or install them, or you ask that we do so, we will use Great Lancashire logistics. Information on delivery and installation options and costs will be provided to you in store before you place your order. You will be able to choose your preferred delivery and/or installation option when you place your order.

6 Carrying out of the services

We will carry out the services by the time or within the period which you and we agree (either in store or in writing). If you and we have agreed no time or period, we will carry out the services within a reasonable time.

7 Charges and payment

7.1   We will let you know the cost of OR basis of calculating the charges for the goods and services (and any extra charges such as delivery OR installation charges) to the fullest extent we can when you place an order with us. We will provide an estimate of lower and higher cost but the final costing is calculated upon completion of the product due to the artistic nature of our designs and sculptures.

7.2   If you do not pay for the goods and fail to return them we may uninstall and collect the goods from you at your expense. We will try to contact you to let you know if we intend to do this.

8 Nature of the goods

8.1   The Consumer Rights Act 2015 gives you certain legal rights (also known as 'statutory rights'). The goods that we provide to you must be as described, fit for purpose and of satisfactory quality. Our wood is ethically sourced from both UK and European forests.

8.2   We are under a legal duty to supply you with goods that are in conformity with this contract.

8.3   Due to the natural nature of our goods, products and sculptures there may be organic changes in the materials due to the exposure to certain environments. All goods must be treated annually with 'Tuckers Wood oil'. All customers are supplied with a fact sheet and are asked to book annually a treatment by one of our wood experts. Failure to treat the product may lead to deterioration and we accept no liability or responsibility should customers not comply with company policy regarding the maintenance and upkeep of the products.

8.4   If we cannot supply certain materials during seasonal fluctuations due to weather and climate issues we may need to substitute them with alternative goods of equal or better standard and value. In this case:

8.4.1   we will let you know if we intend to do this but this may not always be possible; and

8.4.2   you can refuse to accept such substitutes, in which case we will offer you a refund or a replacement and let you know how long such an offer remains open for.

9 Nature of the services

9.1   The Consumer Rights Act 2015 gives you certain legal rights (also known as 'statutory rights'). The services that we provide to you must be carried out with reasonable care and skill. In addition:

9.1.1   where the price has not been agreed upfront, the cost of the services must be reasonable; and

9.1.2   where no time period has been agreed upfront for the provision of the services, we must carry out the services within a reasonable time.

9.2   We are under a legal duty to supply you with services that are in conformity with this contract.

10 Faulty goods or services

10.1   Your legal rights under the Consumer Rights Act 2015 (also known as 'statutory rights'), are set out at the top of this contract. They are a summary of some of your key rights. For more detailed information on your rights and what you should expect from us, please:

10.1.1 speak with us in store and ask for our information sheet: 'Our promises to you if things go wrong';

10.1.2 visit our website: www.tuckerssculptures.com, 'Our promises to you if things go wrong';

10.1.3 contact us using the contact details at the top of this contract; or

10.1.4 visit the Citizens Advice website www.citizensadvice.org.uk or call 0808 223 1133.

10.2 If there is something wrong with the services provided to you, the remedies for services will apply. If there is something wrong with your goods, the remedies for goods will apply. In practice, there may be some overlap between the remedies available to you and we will try to agree the most appropriate course of action with you.

10.3 Nothing in this contract affects your legal rights under the Consumer Rights Act 2015 (also known as 'statutory rights'). You may also have other rights in law.

10.4 If the goods or services we have provided to you are faulty, please contact us using the contact details at the top of this contract.

11 End of the contract

If this contract is ended it will not affect our right to receive any money which you owe to us under this contract.

12 Limitation on our liability

12.1 Except for any legal responsibility that we cannot exclude in law (such as for death or personal injury) or arising under applicable laws relating to the protection of your personal information, we are not legally responsible for any:

12.1.1 losses that were not foreseeable to you and us when the contract was formed;

12.1.2 losses that were not caused by any breach on our part;

12.1.3 business losses; or

12.1.4 losses to non-consumers.

13 Third party rights

No one other than a party to this contract has any right to enforce any term of this contract. However, if a person acquires the goods lawfully from you, you may transfer our guarantee to that person. This also applies where we have provided services in respect of an item you have transferred.

14 Disputes

14.1 We will try to resolve any disputes with you quickly and efficiently. If you are unhappy with the goods you purchased, the services we have provided or any other matter, please contact us as soon as possible using the contact details set out at the top of this contract.

14.2 Our **Complaint Handling Policy** can be accessed on our website at www .tuckerssculptures.com.

14.3 If a dispute cannot be resolved in accordance with our Complaint Handling Policy or you are unhappy with the outcome, you may want to use alternative dispute resolution (**ADR**). ADR is a process for resolving disputes between you and us that does not involve going to court.

14.4 If you do not wish to use ADR or are unhappy with the outcome of ADR, you can still bring court proceedings.

14.5 The laws of England and Wales apply to this contract, although if you are resident elsewhere you will retain the benefit of any mandatory protections given to you by the laws of that country.

14.6 Any disputes will be subject to the non-exclusive jurisdiction of the courts of England and Wales. This means that you can choose whether to bring a claim in the courts of England and Wales or in the courts of another part of the UK in which you live.

Signed by **Nathan Tucker** for and on behalf of Tuckers Wood Ltd	*Nathan Tucker*
	Director
Signed by **Subha Kulendiren**	*Subha Kulendiren*

*   *   *

■ YOUR TURN

Have a go at answering question 2, remembering the guidance on pages 1–2.
- Refer to the structured approach in the SRA's assessment criteria on page 2.
- Create a list of the most salient legal issues raised by this question.
- Timings are important: you will need to prepare and write your answer in one hour.

SQE1 Functioning legal knowledge link
In chapter 9 of *Revise SQE: Contract Law*, we considered the Consumer Rights Act and the remedies for breach of contract. Question 2 demonstrates how your knowledge of this topic could be tested in the context and format of an SQE2 case and matter analysis assessment.

EVALUATING YOUR ANSWER

When you have attempted question 2, mark it yourself against the SQE2 case and matter analysis criteria. Do you think your attempt met the threshold standard?

Now compare your attempt with the following key legal points and two sample answers to question 2. A circled number indicates that commentary is provided for this part of the answer. The commentary explains whether or not the sample satisfies the assessment criteria, and accordingly likely to meet the threshold SQE2 standard.

➡ Key legal points: Question 2

- Explore what must be proved to establish breach of contract in respect of (1) express terms, which are clear, unambiguous and agreed upon by reviewing the contract, and (2) implied terms, ie terms that are implied in the contract under the Consumer Rights Act (CRA) 2015.
- Explore the pre-contract terms/representations made by the parties when the client ordered the product.
- Detail relevant legislation for contracts between Subha and Nathan Tucker: CRA 2015. Explore key terms and breach of those terms.
- Discuss the evidence that Subha is likely to rely upon and whether Nathan Tucker may have any relevant evidence to support his contention regarding the order.
- Explore relief afforded under CRA 2015 and consider what remedy the client is looking for. Does the contract stipulate any process for complaints or disputes?
- Discuss necessity to mitigate loss and consider whether the court will find that Subha has failed to mitigate her loss regarding the deterioration of the furniture.

- Explore preliminary factors including viability, limitation and process. Does Nathan Tucker have any money concerns? How would you find this out? What is the limitation period for contractual matters? What is the process for bringing a claim?
- Necessary requirements in respect of any pre-action protocols, alternatives to litigation and cost consequences. You will need to review the contract for remedies and disputes. You will also need to consider whether there are any relevant protocols which apply to this scenario.

■ SAMPLE ANSWER 1 TO QUESTION 2

The constituent parts of the contract appear in order, namely offer, acceptance, consideration and the intent to create legal relations. In order to pursue TWD for breach of contract we need to establish what the express and implied terms were. It appears from the information supplied by the client that the express terms are likely to be: garden furniture, suitable for use, sourced in the UK and from a sustainable forest. The CRA 2015 contains a number of key terms that are deemed to be implied in contracts between a consumer and a trader. The implied terms will be:

- Section 9: the quality of the goods is satisfactory, namely the furniture should not be faulty or damaged. There is no suggestion that the goods were faulty or damaged upon delivery, but there is an assumption of durability, which the furniture does not seem to have possessed.
- Section 10: the goods are reasonably fit for any particular purpose that the consumer makes known to the trader before buying the goods. Subha would need to establish that she did make it known to Nathan Tucker that she was to use the pieces as furniture both inside and outside her property.
- Section 11: the goods will match the description. The client suggests she discussed the furniture with Nathan Tucker and that a real bond developed. It is clear that the client knew what she wanted the pieces to be used for and that she expected them to be sustainably sourced, durable and from the UK. Again we would need to establish that this was communicated at the time of the order and that the goods do not match their description. We would need independent expert evidence to prove this. ❶

There is also the issue of whether Nathan Tucker's comment that the pieces would withstand the test of time is a term or representation of the pre-contractual statement. If deemed a term, breach would attract damages to put the client back into the position had the contract been performed properly, and if deemed a representation, damages for breach would only be recovered if there is an element of negligent or fraudulent misrepresentation. On the face of the information, we would argue the statement could be deemed a term of the contract on the basis Nathan Tucker thought this to be true. TWD are likely to argue that the statement (if made) was an inducement and made only to convince the client to commission the pieces. ❷

In order to prove breach of contract under the CRA 2015, we will need to obtain statements from the client and her sister, and ensure that they deal with both the express and implied terms of the contract. The client's sister's account, although not independent, will be a useful source of evidence. We will also need to obtain expert evidence from a wood specialist to establish what the client's friend has mentioned to her. It would be prudent to enquire whether Nathan Tucker retained the notes he made on his phone to assist what was noted at the time of the commission. ❸

We can explain to the client that under the CRA 2015 she had a right to have the goods repaired or get a partial refund and that she needs to give TWD an opportunity to do this, but that the burden is on the client to show that the furniture is faulty. The issue here is likely to be that Nathan Tucker was producing a sculpture but the client thought she was commissioning furniture. In order to establish the claim, it is likely we will need statements from the client and her sister, and a wood expert's report on the durability and provenance of the materials used. We should also enquire whether the client has any other documentation appertaining to the order, delivery or installation of the pieces. The client should be advised to retain all the pieces as evidence. ④

The remedy available to the client would be damages for breach of contract: to put the client back into the position they would have been had the contract been performed properly. TWD are likely to argue that the client has not mitigated her losses which is a necessity in a claim for breach of contract, in that she failed to notify them or bring the sculptures inside as soon as she realised that the wood was suffering due to being exposed to external elements. The client also references mental distress and disappointment; however, while the issue with the pieces and the cost incurred is stressful for the client, the general rule is that a party cannot claim for upset and disappointment in a breach of contract claim. ⑤

In order to pursue TWD we would need to establish that the claim is viable and that TWD would be able to satisfy any judgment. A claim for breach of contract must be brought within six years of the date of breach and accordingly the client has ample time. Noting the client's desire to deal with this matter expeditiously, we need to manage the client's expectation and advise that under the CPR we are duty bound to comply with the pre-action protocols. There is no specific protocol relating to contractual claims, but we must follow the practice direction on pre-action conduct and protocols. This requires exchange of information, a letter of claim including concise details, a summary of the facts, the remedy the client requires and the opportunity to respond within a reasonable time (14 days in this case). We also need to attempt to agree an independent expert for analysis of the wood used. We need to ensure the client understands the requirements of complying with the pre-action practice direction prior to the issue of any court proceedings. The contract also mentions ADR, and we should explain the advantages and disadvantages of this to the client. We also need to explain risks involved in litigation and the costs' consequences (namely, loser pays winner's costs). ⑥

COMMENTARY

① The analysis starts by summarising the constituent elements of a contract. Clear, succinct and accurate language is used throughout, and only the relevant sections of CRA 2015 are highlighted in a comprehensive application to the client's situation. There is no need to write or repeat any information that is not relevant. The key is to analyse and apply the law, not write everything known about the particular legal issues.

② This section deals with the potential counter-argument and how this would affect the client's remedy for breach of contract. The candidate has set out the relevant issues clearly and referenced what a possible remedy would be. In mentioning the counter-argument the candidate shows the examiner that they are able to appreciate any argument an opponent may make, and in anticipating it strengthen the client's case.

③ This section deals with evidence. Having discussed and applied the relevant legislation to the client's situation, it is necessary to maintain a client-focused approach and advise the client on how the claim may be evidenced. This shows the examiner that not only does the candidate understand the law but that they are aware of how to evidence a case and what a court may take into consideration. Again this very much leans towards 'application', and feeds into the SQE2 assessment criteria.

④ Again this section refers to Nathan Tucker's potential counter-argument and how important the evidence is to establish the client's position. Not only is documentary evidence necessary but it is also important to understand that the court may actually look at physical evidence. Advising the client to retain this evidence is important and shows the examiner that the candidate understands the bigger picture.

⑤ This section deals with the remedy available to the client and queries mitigation, thus ensuring that the client's expectations are managed and the approach remains client-focused. It is important to provide the client with a remedy but also an answer to the legal problem.

6 This section deals with the professional and ethical obligations to advise the client that irrespective of her desire for a swift resolution, this may not be possible due to the obligation to comply with the CPR. This shows the examiner that the answer meets the SQE2 assessment criteria.

Does this answer meet the threshold?

The sample answer contains a clear and concise assessment of the case and what is needed to take the matter further. It also contains analysis of the issues and details of any remedies which are available, in addition to the limitations of those arguments in respect of the highlighted issues. It is likely to meet the threshold standard for the SQE2 case and matter analysis, as it carefully deals with every aspect of the assessment criteria for case and matter analysis.

Now consider the second sample answer to question 2.

■ SAMPLE ANSWER 2 TO QUESTION 2

Subha should retain the table, chairs and statement bench, as they may be needed as evidence if the case goes to trial. **1**

The law which applies is the Consumer Rights Act 2015: the goods are required to be of satisfactory quality and fit for purpose. This is detailed in the written contract. In order to be successful, Subha must prove that the products were not of satisfactory quality and were not fit for purpose. We could argue that the purpose was to be used as furniture and for use outdoors. However, Nathan is likely to argue that the pieces were fit for use as he explained it was for inside use only, something which the client disputes. **2** The fact that the company supplied and installed the furniture outside – and not inside as Nathan Tucker assumed – should have put them on notice that the client's view was that these were pieces of garden furniture and not indoor sculptures. **3**

We could action under contract law where we would need to prove that there was a breach of contract and that the client has suffered loss. The terms we can rely on under the contract are that the product ordered was:
• Furniture (not a sculpture)
• Suitable for use
• Sourced from wood in the UK
• Of a sustainable nature.

Process
1. We would first issue a letter before claim to inform TWD that we intend to bring an action for the products not being fit for purpose and not being of satisfactory quality.
2. If TWD was not forthcoming to the letter, we would then issue a claim to the court. The claim would be for an amount of £79,500.
3. We would then need to follow the court's steps, including disclosure and potentially a trial. **4**

COMMENTARY
1 The memo starts with a consideration of evidence. The memo needs a structure and detailed consideration of each issue in a logical manner. The candidate needs to remember the SQE2 assessment criteria: this analysis lacks structure and needs to

include a summary of the law which relates to the issues as an introduction. It is a valid point that the items should be retained, but this should be included in a section that discusses evidence.

② This section is too brief and lacks application. Relevant legislation is omitted. There should be a detailed consideration of the relevant legislation which relates to the issue. The candidate should think about the issues, the relevant legislation and how it applies to the client's situation, and then state what their advice would be. The candidate also needs to communicate this in a logical and clear manner to the partner to form the basis of their advice to the client.

③ The contract quite clearly states that the products are delivered and installed by a separate logistics company, so this argument is unlikely to be of assistance.

④ This section is again too brief and lacks any insight into why court proceedings cannot be issued immediately. The examiners are not only looking for the accurate application of law but also the relevant process that must be followed. Suggesting that proceedings can be issued immediately highlights the candidate's lack of understanding or knowledge of the CPR, the overriding objective and the pre-action protocols. There is a lack of any ethical or professional conduct considerations, which is in direct contravention of the SQE2 assessment criteria. The answer does not deal with viability of the claim or any anticipated counter-arguments of the defendant.

Does this answer meet the threshold?

When assessing the second answer against the SQE2 case and matter analysis criteria, it is unlikely that this would meet the threshold standard for SQE2 case and matter analysis. The answer is too brief and fails to detail the relevant legislation in enough detail. There is also a genuine lack of understanding of the litigation process and the CPR.

■ KEY POINT CHECKLIST

This chapter has covered the following key knowledge points:
- The SQE2 assessment criteria for case and matter analysis and how to apply them in the context of dispute resolution in contract.
- A suggested structure for approaching an SQE2 case and matter analysis question.
- Examples of case and matter analysis, which are both likely and unlikely to meet the threshold standard, with full commentary on their strengths and weaknesses.

■ SUMMARY AND REFLECTION

When approaching the SQE2 case and matter analysis, take plenty of time to read the question carefully, think about the legal points the question is asking of you and draw up a short plan to follow so that your answer will be logically and clearly structured.

The examiner will be judging your ability to apply the law both correctly and comprehensively, so as well as pinpointing the relevant law, you will need to explain how it can be applied to the wider context of the client's scenario and the more obvious specific points.

The best way to practise case and matter analysis is to identify the issues in a case and consider what law applies to those issues, then focus on the needs and situation of your client when forming your response.

Now take time to reflect and consider what you might still need to work on, and whether you feel completely confident in your case and matter analysis skills in the context of dispute resolution.

2

Legal research

■ MAKE SURE YOU KNOW

This chapter covers the skill of legal research in the context of dispute resolution. Legal research in dispute resolution is one of the legal skills that may be assessed on day one of the SQE2 assessments (see Introduction for more detail). Bear in mind that the SQE2 assessment can test your knowledge not only of the processes associated with dispute resolution, but also the application of contractual or tortious principles to those processes. Before attempting the questions in this chapter, it is therefore essential that you are familiar with the contents of *Revise SQE: Dispute Resolution*, *Revise SQE: Tort Law* and *Revise SQE: Contract Law*.

This chapter provides examples of how different elements of legal research in the context of contractual and tortious claims could arise in a legal research SQE2 assessment.

■ SQE ASSESSMENT ADVICE

As you work through this chapter, remember to pay particular attention in your revision to:
• selecting relevant information about the legal issue, or the client's problem, from the primary and/or secondary sources provided
• using your findings to substantiate/support your answer to the question asked
• demonstrating an understanding of the client's problem from the client's perspective, eg addressing the client's legal problem, any relevant commercial considerations and/ or the client's priorities, objectives and constraints
• using understandable and simple language to convey facts and information effectively
• using correct legal terminology, where necessary
• identifying the relevant legal principles and applying them correctly to the facts of the client's case
• ensuring your legal analysis is sufficiently detailed in the context of the facts of the case, eg drawing on multiple sources of information to address the legal issue/client's problem effectively
• where relevant, recognising ethical issues and exercising effective judgement in addressing them, in accordance with the SRA principles and rules of professional conduct.

See the Appendix for the SRA's performance indicators in legal research.

■ INTRODUCTION TO LEGAL RESEARCH IN DISPUTE RESOLUTION

The SQE2 assessment in legal research will contain a scenario which could be taken from day-to-day legal practice. For this assessment, you will read a memo or email from a partner which asks you to conduct legal research and provide the correct legal knowledge for them to be able to advise a client, including in your answer the legal authorities supporting this advice. While the question will give you some direction about the areas you need to cover in your legal research, you will be required to apply your knowledge of those areas and your understanding of the resources provided to the scenario, and communicate the relevant information to the partner clearly and concisely in writing. This chapter will provide examples of how you can do this and meet the assessment criteria for SQE2 legal research at the same time.

To succeed in your SQE2 legal research assessment, try to approach the question in a structured manner. The following approach might be useful:

1. First, read through the question and the documentation. Then write down the key facts and legal issues that you feel are relevant to the research and will need to be communicated to the partner.
2. Identify key steps applied in the relevant sources and write your answer to the question.
3. Read through your answer, checking that it addresses the different parts of the SQE2 legal research assessment criteria.

Assessment technique

When structuring your answer, consider what the important issues are and how the law applies to these issues in the client scenario. Read the scenario carefully and deal with each issue in turn so that your conclusion provides client-focused advice, which actually addresses the client's problem.

SQE2 legal research assessment criteria

Try to remember these points as you construct your answer:

Skills

1. Identify and use relevant sources and information.
2. Provide client-focused advice that addresses the client's problem.
3. Use clear, precise, concise and acceptable language.

Application of law

4. Apply the law correctly to the client's situation.
5. Apply the law comprehensively to the client's situation, identifying any ethical and professional conduct issues and exercising judgement to resolve them honestly and with integrity.

In chapter 6 of *Revise SQE: Tort Law*, we considered the duty of care an occupier owed to visitors and non-visitors. Question 1 demonstrates how your knowledge of this topic could be tested in the context and format of an SQE2 legal research assessment.

The sample questions in the chapter include six sources for you to consider, but bear in mind that the SQE2 assessment might include up to eight sources.

■ QUESTION 1

Email to candidate

From: Partner
Sent: 2 March 202#
To: Candidate
Subject: Samara McDonald

A new client, Samara McDonald, telephoned me today. She would like some advice on whether or not she is able to bring a claim for personal injury following an incident at a work night out.

Samara explained that her company booked a restaurant for the staff in the town centre (Bistro Cuisine) for 7 PM and about 30 colleagues attended. After the meal at about 10 PM, her boss suggested they all go to the local pub Lime Street Towers, which is known for its architectural design dating back to the 19th century. The pub has recently been renovated and features stunning original features as well as some additional modern features, such as spiral staircases. Samara says that most of her colleagues went to the pub and that there was an amount of money put behind the bar by her boss for drinks. She says she drank two glasses of wine at the restaurant and then had two large gin and tonics in the pub but did not feel drunk. She had eaten a starter, main course and dessert at the restaurant.

At about midnight, some of her colleagues decided to head home. Samara was on the first floor of the pub which has a mezzanine level, accessed by a spiral staircase. As they approached the spiral staircase, one of her colleagues joked with her and dared her to slide down the banister of the spiral staircase. Samara decided to take her up on the challenge and slid down the banister. Unfortunately, halfway down the banister she lost her balance and fell. She was badly injured: an ambulance was called and she was taken to the local hospital where she was diagnosed with a hip and shoulder fracture. She underwent surgery and is currently recuperating. She has been unable to work and has been advised she may need further surgery, depending on how she recovers from her injuries.

Samara feels strongly that the spiral staircase is dangerous: (1) the banisters are made from very slippery metal, which is an allurement to customers; (2) there are no warning signs about the height nor signs discouraging customers from sliding down them. Samara categorically states that she was not drunk at the time of the accident and thinks that the owners have been negligent in not placing a notice preventing customers from climbing or sliding down the banisters. Indeed she recalls a group of men at the top of the spiral staircase pretending to slide down the banister when she and her colleagues first arrived at the pub.

Samara would like to know whether she is able to bring a claim for personal injury against the owners of the pub.

Could you please research the answer to this question, using the sources provided? Report back to me so that I can prepare my advice to Samara.

I would like you to include, for my reference, your legal reasoning, mentioning any key sources or authorities.

Many thanks

Partner

Note to candidates:

Given the time constraints of this assessment, we have not provided the full text of some primary sources. Where the full text of a primary source is not provided, candidates may nevertheless cite the primary source on the basis it is referred to in one or more of the secondary sources provided and the full text can be checked at a later date.

Information displayed is as obtained on the date of search, for example purposes only. Information herein is not to be relied upon outside of the purposes of this sample question.

Attachments

You have been provided with the following sources listed alphabetically in order of source name. The order of presentation is not intended as a guide to the order in which they should be consulted.

PLEASE NOTE THAT PART OR ALL OF SOME OF THESE SOURCES MAY NOT BE RELEVANT TO ANSWERING THE QUESTION.

1. Defective Premises Act 1972, c 35 s 4
2. *Geary v JD Wetherspoon plc* [2011] EWHC 1506 (QB)
3. *James v White Lion Hotel (a partnership)* [2021] EWCA Civ 31
4. Law Reform (Contributory Negligence) Act 1945, c 28 s 1
5. Occupiers' Liability Act 1957, c 31 s 2
6. Occupiers' Liability Act 1984, c 3 s 1.

*   *   *

Source 1

Contains public sector information licensed under the Open Government Licence v3.0.

Defective Premises Act 1972, c 35 s 4

4 Landlord's duty of care in virtue of obligation or right to repair premises demised

(1) Where premises are let under a tenancy which puts on the landlord an obligation to the tenant for the maintenance or repair of the premises, the landlord owes to all persons who might reasonably be expected to be affected by defects in the state of the premises a duty to take such care as is reasonable in all the circumstances to see that they are reasonably safe from personal injury or from damage to their property caused by a relevant defect.

(2) The said duty is owed if the landlord knows (whether as the result of being notified by the tenant or otherwise) or if he ought in all the circumstances to have known of the relevant defect.

(3) In this section 'relevant defect' means a defect in the state of the premises existing at or after the material time and arising from, or continuing because of, an act or omission by the landlord which constitutes or would if he had had notice of the defect, have constituted a failure by him to carry out his obligation to the tenant for the maintenance or repair of the premises; and for the purposes of the foregoing provision 'the material time' means—

    (a) where the tenancy commenced before this Act, the commencement of this Act; and

    (b) in all other cases, the earliest of the following times, that is to say—

(i)   the time when the tenancy commences;

(ii) the time when the tenancy agreement is entered into;

(iii) the time when possession is taken of the premises in contemplation of the letting.

(4) Where premises are let under a tenancy which expressly or impliedly gives the landlord the right to enter the premises to carry out any description of maintenance or repair of the premises, then, as from the time when he first is, or by notice or otherwise can put himself, in a position to exercise the right and so long as he is or can put himself in that position, he shall be treated for the purposes of subsections (1) to (3) above (but for no other purpose) as if he were under an obligation to the tenant for that description of maintenance or repair of the premises; but the landlord shall not owe the tenant any duty by virtue of this subsection in respect of any defect in the state of the premises arising from, or continuing because of, a failure to carry out an obligation expressly imposed on the tenant by the tenancy.

(5) For the purposes of this section obligations imposed or rights given by any enactment in virtue of a tenancy shall be treated as imposed or given by the tenancy.

(6) This section applies to a right of occupation given by contract or any enactment and not amounting to a tenancy as if the right were a tenancy, and 'tenancy' and cognate expressions shall be construed accordingly.

* * *

Source 2

Contains public sector information licensed under the Open Government Licence v3.0.

Geary v JD Wetherspoon plc [2011] EWHC 1506 (QB)

2   … On the evening of 29 March 2007, the claimant, Mrs Ruth Geary, had been drinking with some work colleagues at *The Union Rooms*, a pub in Newcastle City Centre, close to the station, which is owned and operated by the defendant. The premises had formerly been a gentleman's club. One of the original features of the building, which was deliberately left untouched by the refurbishment, was a grand open staircase in the centre of the building, with sweeping banisters on both sides, rising to a half-landing and then turning upwards on either side to the first floor. On her way out with her colleagues, the claimant hoisted herself onto the left banister with the intention of sliding down it. Unfortunately she fell backwards and landed on the marble floor just less than 4 metres below. She sustained a fracture to her spine, resulting in tetraplegia.

3   In March 2010, the claimant issued proceedings against the defendant, claiming damages for personal injury. The principal claim was put by way of negligence, that is to say as a breach of an alleged common law duty of care …

4   … the issues between the parties were relatively straightforward. In essence, they concerned the existence or otherwise of the duty of care alleged by the claimant. They can perhaps be summarised as follows:

(a) Was there a voluntary assumption of an obvious and inherent risk by the claimant, in circumstances which would negate any liability on the part of the defendant?

(b) Was there an assumption of responsibility by the defendant to the claimant?

32   It was submitted on behalf of the defendant that the claimant voluntarily assumed the obvious risk inherent in sliding down open banisters, which, on the far side, had a long drop to the marble floor below. In consequence, the defendant maintains that they can have no liability in law to the claimant, whether as alleged or at all. The claimant maintains that her own conduct, while plainly relevant to issues of contributory negligence, could not amount to a defence in law.

45   In my view, there is no difference in principle between *Tomlinson* and the present case. Similarly, I also conclude that this case is indistinguishable from *Poppleton*. Both Mr Poppleton and the claimant deliberately took the risk that they might fall. Neither intended to fall but, due to a momentary misjudgement, they both did. And in both cases the defendant had taken some steps to deal with the problem (in *Poppleton* they had provided safety mats, here they had warned would-be sliders away from the banisters), and could not reasonably be expected to do more.

46   In light of the claimant's candid evidence about the obvious risk that she ran, it seems to me that the principle of voluntary assumption of risk, set out in the cases noted above, is fatal to her claim. The claimant freely chose to do something which she knew to be dangerous. Because of the conversations about 'Mary Poppins', there was even a degree of pre-planning. She knew that sliding down the banisters was not permitted, but she chose to do it anyway. She was therefore the author of her own misfortune. The defendant owed no duty to protect her from such an obvious and inherent risk. She made a genuine and informed choice and the risk that she chose to run materialised with tragic consequences.

47   In those circumstances, I consider that, on the law, I am bound to find that this claim must fail. It would be contrary to binding authority to do otherwise.

77   For the reasons set out above, I consider that no relevant duty of care was owed by the defendant to the claimant. In those circumstances it is unnecessary for me to go on to consider questions of breach. I have also concluded that, even if both duty and breach had been made out, the probability must be that they were non-causative, and that the claimant would have slid anyway, even if the banister had been at normal height.

* * *

Source 3

James v White Lion Hotel (a partnership) [2021] EWCA Civ 31

2   On 5 July 2015, the deceased, aged 41, was staying in a twin room on the second floor of *The White Lion Hotel*, Upton-upon-Severn, Worcester. The hotel is owned and operated by Jonathan Lear and his wife, Christine Lear, who trade as a partnership (the appellant). The deceased and his travelling companion, Ms Palfreyman, were attending a wedding. They returned to the hotel room following the wedding. Ms Palfreyman was asleep on the single bed next to the window, when, at around 2.46 AM, the deceased fell to his death from the sash window of the room. He landed on the pavement approximately nine metres from the window. His body was discovered at around 4 AM. The deceased was five foot seven inches tall and weighed 83 kilograms.

3   Following an investigation into the accident, the appellant was prosecuted for offences contrary to section 3 of the Health and Safety at Work Act 1974 ('the 1974 Act'). A guilty plea was entered upon an agreed basis.

4   The claim is brought pursuant to section 2 of the Occupiers' Liability Act 1957 ('the 1957 Act') alleging a failure to take reasonable care for the safety of the deceased. The judge found that the appellant was in breach of the common duty of care pursuant to section 2 of the 1957 Act in failing to take reasonable care for the safety of the deceased in using the room but made a finding of 60% contributory negligence.

5   There is no appeal as to the findings of fact made by the judge nor as to the finding of 60% contributory negligence. The points raised in the appeal are issues of law. The essence of the appeal is contained in the first ground, namely that the judge, having found that the deceased had chosen to sit on the window sill, part out of the window, and had recognised and accepted the risk of falling from the window due to leaning too far out or losing his balance, erred in law in failing to apply the principle that a person of full age and capacity who chooses to run an obvious risk cannot found an action against a defendant on the basis that the latter has either permitted him to do so, or not prevented him from so doing. In so doing the judge failed to apply the ratio of *Tomlinson v Congleton Borough Council* [2004] 1 AC 46, *Edwards v Sutton London Borough Council* [2016] EWCA Civ 1005 and *Geary v JD Weatherspoon plc* [2011] EWHC 1506 (QB).

6   Further grounds of appeal are pursued, which raise the questions:
    (i)   does section 2(5) of the 1957 Act apply, such that the appellant had no obligation to the deceased in respect of the risk of falling from the window?
    (ii) did the judge err in holding that, as a matter of law, an occupier who is in breach of his statutory duty under section 3(1) of the 1974 Act was *ipso facto* in breach of his duty to a visitor under the 1957 Act?

74 ... the conclusions drawn by the judge at [42] as to the existence of the appellant's duty to the deceased, a lawful visitor, the foreseeable risk of serious injury due to the state of the premises, the absence of social value of the activity leading to the risk and the minimal cost of preventative measures are unassailable. In my judgment they are findings which provide a sound factual basis for a determination that the appellant breached its section 2 common duty of care to the deceased.

77 ... consideration of these authorities does not provide unequivocal support for the proposition contended for by the appellant.

84 Separate from the considerations above, there are a number of factual features, which distinguish this case from those of *Edwards*, *Tomlinson* and *Geary*:
    (i)   The lower sash window was defective. No defect was present in the ornamental bridge in *Edwards*, the body of water in *Tomlinson*, nor the banister in *Geary*.
    (ii) In this case, the judge found that a risk assessment would have made a critical difference. In *Edwards* McCombe LJ found that a risk assessment would have done no more than state the obvious.
    (iii) The risk of injury was foreseeable. In *Edwards* the risk was remote and had never previously materialised.
    (iv) The social value lost by taking preventative measures was low given that the top sash window could still be opened. In *Edwards*, side barriers would have significantly altered the character of the ornamental bridge, in *Tomlinson* destroying the beaches would have been at huge social cost.
    (v)   The financial costs of fitting the window restrictors was negligible (£7 or £8 per window). The same cannot be said of the preventative measures in *Edwards* or *Tomlinson*.

86 In my judgment, there is a material difference between a visitor to a park, even a pub, and a guest in a hotel. During the time the guest is in the hotel room it is a 'home from home'. The guest in the room may be tired, off-guard, relaxing and may well have had more than a little to drink. Despite notices to the contrary he

may be tempted to smoke out of the window and in hot weather the guest will want fresh air, particularly, as in this case, in a room with no air conditioning. As the judge observed, these are 'facts of life' for any hotelier. These are normal activities.

87 Contrast these facts with the 'activities' contemplated in *Tomlinson*. Lord Hoffman at [45] observed that 'it will be extremely rare for an occupier of land to be under a duty to prevent people from taking risks which are inherent in the activities they freely choose to undertake upon the land. If people want to climb mountains, go hang gliding or swim or dive in ponds or lakes, that is their affair'. These activities go far beyond those involved in the ordinary occupation of a hotel room.

88 For the reasons given, I do not accept the appellant's primary contention. There is no absolute principle that a visitor of full age and capacity who chooses to run an obvious risk cannot found an action against an occupier on the basis that the latter has either permitted him so to do, or not prevented him from so doing. Subject to the opinions of King LJ and Elisabeth Laing LJ, I would dismiss this ground of appeal.

99 Accordingly, for the reasons given, and subject to the views of King LJ and Elisabeth Laing LJ, I do not accede to the appellant's appeal in respect of section 2(5) of the 1957 Act.

100 Section 47(1)(a) of the 1974 Act states that:

'(1) Nothing in this Part shall be construed—
   (a) as conferring a right of action in any civil proceedings in respect of any failure to comply with any duty imposed by sections 2 to 7 or any contravention of section 8; ...'

101 Given the clear wording of this section, I am unable to accept the conclusion of the judge at [92] that unless the conviction is challenged on its facts, civil liability does axiomatically follow, as a matter of law. I accept the need for coherence and consistency as between the civil and criminal law, which apply to the same set of facts, but those facts have to be explored in order to decide whether, and if so, how, a criminal conviction relates to civil liability. At the civil trial, there was no attempt to go behind the criminal conviction nor the basis of plea. In my judgment, account could and should be taken of the fact of the conviction and the basis upon which the plea of guilty was entered. As to the weight to be attached to the conviction and any basis of plea, that will depend upon the facts of each case. In this case, the risk was directly relevant to the tragic events which materialised. It does not follow that in every case such a chain of causation will be made out. I accept that the assessment pursuant to section 3 of the 1984 Act and section 2 of the 1957 Act was in key respects the same. It is important that the civil and criminal law should be internally consistent. That said, each assessment will be fact-specific and it does not follow, and I do not find, that civil liability axiomatically follows an unchallenged criminal conviction in civil proceedings.

105 It follows, and subject to the opinions of King LJ and Elisabeth Laing LJ, I accept the appellant's contention that the judge erred in holding that, as a matter of law, an occupier who was in breach of his statutory duty under section 3(1) of the 1974 Act was *ipso facto* in breach of his duty to a visitor under the 1957 Act.

© Crown copyright

*   *   *

Source 4

Contains public sector information licensed under the Open Government Licence v3.0.

Law Reform (Contributory Negligence) Act 1945, c 28 s 1

1 Apportionment of liability in case of contributory negligence

(1) Where any person suffers damage as the result partly of his own fault and partly of the fault of any other person or persons, a claim in respect of that damage shall not be defeated by reason of the fault of the person suffering the damage, but the damages recoverable in respect thereof shall be reduced to such extent as the court thinks just and equitable having regard to the claimant's share in the responsibility for the damage:
Provided that—
  (a) this subsection shall not operate to defeat any defence arising under a contract;
  (b) where any contract or enactment providing for the limitation of liability is applicable to the claim, the amount of damages recoverable by the claimant by virtue of this subsection shall not exceed the maximum limit so applicable.

(2) Where damages are recoverable by any person by virtue of the foregoing subsection subject to such reduction as is therein mentioned, the court shall find and record the total damages which would have been recoverable if the claimant had not been at fault.

(3) ...

(4) ...

(5) Where, in any case to which subsection (1) of this section applies, one of the persons at fault avoids liability to any other such person or his personal representative by pleading the Limitation Act 1939, or any other enactment limiting the time within which proceedings may be taken, he shall not be entitled to recover any damages ... from that other person or representative by virtue of the said subsection.

(6) Where any case to which subsection (1) of this section applies is tried with a jury, the jury shall determine the total damages which would have been recoverable if the claimant had not been at fault and the extent to which those damages are to be reduced.

*   *   *

Source 5

Contains public sector information licensed under the Open Government Licence v3.0.

Occupiers' Liability Act 1957, c 31 s 2

2 Extent of occupier's ordinary duty

(1) An occupier of premises owes the same duty, the 'common duty of care', to all his visitors, except in so far as he is free to and does extend, restrict, modify or exclude his duty to any visitor or visitors by agreement or otherwise.

(2) The common duty of care is a duty to take such care as in all the circumstances of the case is reasonable to see that the visitor will be reasonably safe in using the premises for the purposes for which he is invited or permitted by the occupier to be there.

(3) The circumstances relevant for the present purpose include the degree of care, and of want of care, which would ordinarily be looked for in such a visitor, so that (for example) in proper cases—

(a) an occupier must be prepared for children to be less careful than adults; and

(b) an occupier may expect that a person, in the exercise of his calling, will appreciate and guard against any special risks ordinarily incident to it, so far as the occupier leaves him free to do so.

(4) In determining whether the occupier of premises has discharged the common duty of care to a visitor, regard is to be had to all the circumstances, so that (for example)—

(a) where damage is caused to a visitor by a danger of which he had been warned by the occupier, the warning is not to be treated without more as absolving the occupier from liability, unless in all the circumstances it was enough to enable the visitor to be reasonably safe; and

(b) where damage is caused to a visitor by a danger due to the faulty execution of any work of construction, maintenance or repair by an independent contractor employed by the occupier, the occupier is not to be treated without more as answerable for the danger if in all the circumstances he had acted reasonably in entrusting the work to an independent contractor and had taken such steps (if any) as he reasonably ought in order to satisfy himself that the contractor was competent and that the work had been properly done.

(5) The common duty of care does not impose on an occupier any obligation to a visitor in respect of risks willingly accepted as his by the visitor (the question whether a risk was so accepted to be decided on the same principles as in other cases in which one person owes a duty of care to another).

(6) For the purposes of this section, persons who enter premises for any purpose in the exercise of a right conferred by law are to be treated as permitted by the occupier to be there for that purpose, whether they in fact have his permission or not.

* * *

Source 6

Occupiers' Liability Act 1984, c 3 s 1

1 Duty of occupier to persons other than his visitors

(1) The rules enacted by this section shall have effect, in place of the rules of the common law, to determine—

(a) whether any duty is owed by a person as occupier of premises to persons other than his visitors in respect of any risk of their suffering injury on the premises by reason of any danger due to the state of the premises or to things done or omitted to be done on them; and

(b) if so, what that duty is.

(2) For the purposes of this section, the persons who are to be treated respectively as an occupier of any premises (which, for those purposes, include any fixed or movable structure) and as his visitors are—

    (a) any person who owes in relation to the premises the duty referred to in section 2 of the Occupiers' Liability Act 1957 (the common duty of care), and

    (b) those who are his visitors for the purposes of that duty.

(3) An occupier of premises owes a duty to another (not being his visitor) in respect of any such risk as is referred to in subsection (1) above if—

    (a) he is aware of the danger or has reasonable grounds to believe that it exists;

    (b) he knows or has reasonable grounds to believe that the other is in the vicinity of the danger concerned or that he may come into the vicinity of the danger (in either case, whether the other has lawful authority for being in that vicinity or not); and

    (c) the risk is one against which, in all the circumstances of the case, he may reasonably be expected to offer the other some protection.

(4) Where, by virtue of this section, an occupier of premises owes a duty to another in respect of such a risk, the duty is to take such care as is reasonable in all the circumstances of the case to see that he does not suffer injury on the premises by reason of the danger concerned.

(5) Any duty owed by virtue of this section in respect of a risk may, in an appropriate case, be discharged by taking such steps as are reasonable in all the circumstances of the case to give warning of the danger concerned or to discourage persons from incurring the risk.

(6) No duty is owed by virtue of this section to any person in respect of risks willingly accepted as his by that person (the question whether a risk was so accepted to be decided on the same principles as in other cases in which one person owes a duty of care to another).

[F1 (6A) At any time when the right conferred by section 2(1) of the Countryside and Rights of Way Act 2000 is exercisable in relation to land which is access land for the purposes of Part I of that Act, an occupier of the land owes (subject to subsection (6C) below) no duty by virtue of this section to any person in respect of—

    (a) a risk resulting from the existence of any natural feature of the landscape, or any river, stream, ditch or pond whether or not a natural feature, or

    (b) a risk of that person suffering injury when passing over, under or through any wall, fence or gate, except by proper use of the gate or of a stile.

[F2 (6AA) Where the land is coastal margin for the purposes of Part 1 of that Act (including any land treated as coastal margin by virtue of section 16 of that Act), subsection (6A) has effect as if for paragraphs (a) and (b) of that subsection there were substituted 'a risk resulting from the existence of any physical feature (whether of the landscape or otherwise)'.]

(6B) For the purposes of subsection (6A) above, any plant, shrub or tree, of whatever origin, is to be regarded as a natural feature of the landscape.

(6C) Subsection (6A) does not prevent an occupier from owing a duty by virtue of this section in respect of any risk where the danger concerned is due to anything done by the occupier—

    (a) with the intention of creating that risk, or

    (b) being reckless as to whether that risk is created.]

(7) No duty is owed by virtue of this section to persons using the highway, and this section does not affect any duty owed to such persons.

(8) Where a person owes a duty by virtue of this section, he does not, by reason of any breach of the duty, incur any liability in respect of any loss of or damage to property.

(9) In this section—

    • 'highway' means any part of a highway other than a ferry or waterway;

- 'injury' means anything resulting in death or personal injury, including any disease and any impairment of physical or mental condition; and
- 'movable structure' includes any vessel, vehicle or aircraft.

© Crown copyright

*   *   *

■ YOUR TURN

Have a go at answering question 1, remembering the guidance on pages 20–21.
- Remember the structured approach in the SRA's assessment criteria on page 21.
- Create a list of the relevant answers to the legal points provided in the sources and information, remembering to use primary sources over secondary sources wherever possible (for this question, only primary sources were provided).
- Timings are important: you will need to prepare and write your answer in one hour.

EVALUATING YOUR ANSWER

When you have attempted question 1, mark it yourself against the SQE2 legal research assessment criteria. Do you think your attempt met the threshold standard?

Now compare your attempt with the following key legal points and two sample answers to question 1. A circled number indicates that commentary is provided for this part of the answer. The commentary explains whether or not the sample satisfies the assessment criteria, and accordingly likely to meet the threshold SQE2 standard.

SQE1 Functioning legal knowledge link
Remember from chapter 6 of *Revise SQE: Tort Law* that s 1(1) of the Occupiers' Liability Act 1957 regulates the duty which an *occupier* of premises owes to his visitors, in respect of dangers due to the state of the premises or to things done or omitted to be done on them.

➡Key legal points: Question 1

In this assessment, part, or all, of the following sources are relevant to the question:

- *Geary v JD Wetherspoon plc* [2011] EWHC 1506 (QB)
- *James v White Lion Hotel (a partnership)* [2021] EWCA Civ 31
- Law Reform (Contributory Negligence) Act 1945, c 28 s 1
- Occupiers' Liability Act 1957, c 31 s 2
- Occupiers' Liability Act 1984, c 3 s 1.

The following source is not relevant to the question:

- Defective Premises Act 1972, c 35 s 4.

Key legal points include the following:

- The relevant legislation applicable depends on whether the client is viewed as a visitor or trespasser. If the client is a visitor to the premises, the relevant legislation is Occupiers' Liability Act (OLA) 1957. If the client is a non-visitor, the relevant legislation is Occupiers' Liability Act (OLA) 1984.

- It is necessary to consider the definitions under the legislation and to deal with preliminary points such as premises, control and the definition of a visitor under OLA 1957. It is likely Samara will be classified as a visitor under OLA 1957, but it is important to consider whether at any point she exceeds her permission and becomes a trespasser under OLA 1984.
- Remember that liability under the Acts will arise due to the state of the premises. Liability attaches due to the state of the premises and not due to the client's actions on the premises. Section 2(2) of OLA 1957 makes this clear, confirming that the common law duty of care is a duty to ensure visitors are reasonably safe in using the premises.
- Ensure that you deal with the client's actions and assess them in light of the liability under the legislation. Consider that all cases turn on their own facts. Use the case law presented to compare the actions of the client. In order to establish liability, the client will need to prove there was a duty, that it was breached and that the breach led to her injury.
- Ensure that you discuss whether there are any defences available to the potential defendant. The most relevant defences may be contributory negligence and *volenti*. Remember that *volenti* is a complete defence. However, if liability is established by the court, they will then consider whether the client has contributed to her injuries and may reduce her damages by a percentage to reflect that contribution.

■ SAMPLE ANSWER 1 TO QUESTION 1

The client seeks advice relating to whether there is an actionable claim against Lime Street Towers. The client was a visitor to the premises and as such should be afforded the protection of the Occupiers' Liability Act 1957 (OLA 1957). OLA 1957 seeks to protect lawful visitors from injury. I have no reason to suspect the client will not be afforded the status of visitor. She was there with her colleagues, she purchased drinks and it is a public place. **❶**

An occupier must have sufficient control over the premises. I have no reason to suspect that the proprietors of the pub would not be considered occupiers. They have control over who they allow on their premises and who they sell alcohol to. **❷**

Under s 2(2) OLA 1957, the occupiers owe visitors a duty of care, which is to take such care as in all the circumstances of the case is reasonable to see that the visitor will be reasonably safe in using the premises for the purposes for which he is invited or permitted by the occupier to be there. Importantly, the client was permitted to be on the premises to purchase alcohol and enjoy a social gathering, but arguably she was not permitted to be there to slide down the spiral staircase. **❸**

The standard of care is similar to that of negligence, so for example if visitors are vulnerable they can expect the occupier to take steps to guard against any vulnerability. However, this is not the case here. Under s 2(4)a of OLA 1957, there is some protection for occupiers where claimants have been warned about the danger. The warning will not, however, absolve an occupier from liability unless in all the circumstances it was enough to enable the visitor to be reasonably safe. This means that the court will consider the type of danger and the warning given, and ascertain whether the warning was enough to keep the visitor reasonably safe. The pub had not placed any warnings near the spiral staircase, and we do not know whether there have been any previous accidents, which would perhaps have prompted the owners of the pub to place warning signs there. Where the danger is obvious, the occupier need not warn against it and can rely upon the openly apparent risk posed by the danger to alert the claimant to the potential danger. In this case, the occupier could argue that it is an obvious danger to sit on a banister and try to slide down it, and on that basis they could potentially defeat a claim on the basis that they have not breached their duty. Therefore, it is possible that the pub would have a full defence to the claim if it was brought under OLA 1957. ④

Turning to OLA 1984, this law relates to non-visitors. We have already established that the client was a visitor when she entered the pub to buy a drink and socialise with her friends, as she would have had both express and implied permission to be on the premises. However, it is arguable that the minute that she exceeds her permission to be on the premises, namely the minute that she sits on the banister of the spiral staircase and tries to slide down it, she has exceeded her permission to be on the premises. There is potential for a claim under OLA 1984. However, a duty of care does not automatically arise under this Act, and s 1(3) outlines the three conditions that have to be satisfied. For this case: (1) the occupier had to be aware of the danger or have reasonable grounds to believe it existed, (2) the occupier had to believe or had reasonable grounds to believe that customers were actively trying to slide down the spiral staircase, and (3) the risk must have been so high that in all circumstances the occupiers may reasonably have been expected to offer some protection. Again the claim is likely to fail on the basis that a spiral staircase is not a danger in itself. The accident did not occur due to the state of the premises but what the client chose to do on the premises. ⑤

If the court does entertain the claim, the occupier could have a complete defence on the basis of *volenti*. Potentially, the pub could argue that the claimant voluntarily accepted the risk of injuring herself when she jumped up on the banister and tried to slide down the spiral staircase. In order to defend the claim, the occupier will need to establish capacity (clearly, she has this), knowledge and willingness (arguably an adult knows the dangers of sliding down a banister), and agreement (express or implied – the risk being so obvious she could be deemed to have consented to it the moment she sat on the banister). ⑥

Furthermore, if the court finds the defendant primarily at fault, the claimant may be found to have contributed to her injuries (through contributory negligence – see the Law Reform (Contributory Negligence) Act 1945) and her damages could be reduced accordingly. ⑦

The case of *James v White Lion Hotel (a partnership)* [2021] illustrates that knowledge and acceptance of breach of duty do not preclude a finding of breach of duty. However, in the circumstances it is unlikely a court would find a spiral staircase to be synonymous with an open sash window – one can expect a hotel guest to open and lean out of a window, but one would not expect a pub customer to slide down a banister. Therefore, although this case appears very similar (there was a finding of liability but damages were reduced by 60% to take into account the claimant's acceptance of risk in sitting on the window sill, partly out of the window), it should be recognised that the case does not assist the client. ⑧

The case of *Geary v JD Wetherspoon plc* [2011] suggests that while one could contemplate a claim under OLA 1957 and/or OLA 1984, it is unlikely that the court would conclude the defendant was in breach of duty under either Act as the premises were neither defective nor unsafe, and the client choose to and accepted the risk of injury when she sat on the banister and slid down it. Even if the court finds breach under OLA 1957, the defendant may have a full defence on the basis of *volenti*. Also, the occupier could argue no duty of care under OLA 1984 (if the client is deemed a trespasser when she exceeded her permission by sitting and sliding down the banister), as a spiral staircase is not a danger and there was no need to put up warning signs. Also the client should be aware of any arguments of contributory negligence on the part of the claimant if the court find primary liability attaches. ⑨

My recommendation would be to advise the client that the chances of successfully bringing a claim against Lime Street Towers are less than favourable.

I have based my advice on OLA 1957 and OLA 1984, the Law Reform (Contributory Negligence) Act 1945 and the cases of *James v White Lion Hotel (a partnership)* [2021] and *Geary v JD Wetherspoon plc* [2011]. The Defective Premises Act 1972 is not relevant as this relates to buildings that are defective in some way, where the defect has caused injury to the claimant. The staircase was not defective. ⑩

COMMENTARY

① The relevant Act is OLA 1957. Any claim brought for personal injury would be done so under OLA 1957, so the candidate has correctly included the initial reference to the definition of duty owed to the client under the Act.

② It is important for the candidate to illustrate that they understand the definitions under the Act. These are not included in the research documents, but this is knowledge you should be aware of from the tort law practice area in SQE1 (check **Revise SQE: Tort Law** if you want to review this topic).

③ This paragraph details the definition under the Act but also shows evidence of application, which satisfies the SQE2 assessment criteria. Using the scenario facts and applying the law is a requirement, so that the candidate not only shows their understanding but also assesses the information and forms an opinion on the limitations of any prospective claim under the Act.

④ Here the candidate carefully considers the issues and applies logic and reasoning to the scenario. It may be logical to expect a warning notice on the spiral staircase, but in previous cases the courts have considered that some dangers are so obvious that no warning is necessary. The candidate clearly applies the law and advises that the defendant might have a full defence.

⑤ Having considered OLA 1957, the candidate correctly moves on to OLA 1984, and considers whether the client exceeded her permission and became a trespasser once she climbed onto the banister. Note the logical structure of the answer here, and the correct and comprehensive application of s 1(3) to the facts of the case, which addresses the SQE2's assessment criteria.

⑥ It is important to consider any defences, and *volenti* is relevant here. The research documents do not make reference to defences, but again you should have this knowledge from the tort law practice area in SQE1. Here the candidate tries to manage the client's expectations and advises what defences are relevant.

⑦ When considering defences it is always appropriate to consider contributory negligence. This is particularly important in this case. The candidate makes correct reference to the Law Reform (Contributory Negligence) Act 1945 as relevant to this case.

⑧ Here the candidate considers one of the cases provided and distinguishes it as appropriate. Again this shows that the candidate is capable of assessing and applying relevant information, and also analysing whether the court will heed the same.

⑨ This second case is most similar to the client's case. It is correctly and carefully considered and used to form the candidate's advice to the client.

⑩ This final paragraph highlights the sources used, thus illustrating that the candidate was aware there was irrelevant material and was able to distinguish the relevant from the irrelevant.

Does this answer meet the threshold?

The sample answer contains all of the information that the client requires and that the candidate has been asked to provide. It discusses the relevant legislation and how this applies to the scenario, and reflects upon the cases which are pertinent to the client's circumstances. It is clear, succinct and legally correct. It is therefore likely to meet the threshold standard for SQE2 legal research.

Now consider the second sample answer to question 1.

■ SAMPLE ANSWER 2 TO QUESTION 1

The client could bring a claim under the Occupiers' Liability Act 1957 (OLA 1957), the Occupiers' Liability Act 1984 (OLA 1984) and also the Defective Premises Act 1972. **❶**

The Occupiers' Liability Acts protect visitors and trespassers to premises. The client was a visitor at the time of her accident. She had gone to the pub with colleagues and was enjoying a drink.

The client was injured when she slid down the banister at the pub. The building is old, and as it is a pub the owners should expect customers to be drinking alcohol. This means that their reasoning becomes altered. **❷**

The pub should have placed warning signs on the staircase or roped it off so as to prevent its customers trying to slide down it. The client has been injured due to the state of the premises. **❸**

The client would also need to plead the OLA 1984. If the court does not accept she was a visitor, she could claim damages as a trespasser. She may be considered to have become a trespasser when she climbed onto the banister. The 1984 Act suggests that the pub should have been aware of the danger and displayed signs to customers to warn them of the danger posed by the staircase. It is evident that other people were enticed to attempt to slide down the banister, as the client mentions that when she first arrived at the pub a group of men were joking about the same thing. It seems a recipe for disaster or an accident waiting to happen, which could have been avoided by the pub roping off the banister or placing warning signs. **❹**

The Defective Premises Act 1972 is relevant as it is arguable that the pub premises are defective. A dangerous staircase could lead to a successful claim be brought by the client. **❺**

The case of *Geary* can be distinguished as the claimant in that case was deemed to be a trespasser. This would suggest that the rightful Act would be OLA 1957, as the client was a paying customer and a visitor under that Act. **❻**

The case of *James v White Lion* helps the client and shows that although the client accepted the danger of the staircase, she may be found 60% at fault. **❼**

I recommend we encourage the client to bring a claim under all three Acts mentioned, but explain that she may be found contributorily negligent as she climbed onto the banister and accepted some risk. **❽**

COMMENTARY

❶ This is not correct. Technically a claim can be brought under a variety of legislation, but the Defective Premises Act is not relevant as this relates to buildings that are defective in some way (see point 5 below for more detail). The OLA 1957 and the OLA 1984 are the relevant legislation for this case.

❷ While it is true that alcohol affects reasoning, this in itself does not make the staircase defective nor the proprietors responsible for the client's actions. Remember that if the court finds that liability attaches to the proprietors, only then will they consider whether the client has contributed to her injuries. In this respect the amount of alcohol the client had consumed may be relevant.

❸ This is not correct. Section 2(2) of OLA 57 states that a duty is owed by an occupier to take such care as is reasonable in the circumstances, to see that visitors will be reasonably safe in using the premises for the purposes for which they are invited or permitted by the occupier to be there. Arguably the client is permitted to be there to consume alcohol and socialise with her friends, but not to sit on and slide down the banister. The state of the premises is not the cause of the client's injuries, so the candidate has incorrectly applied the law here.

4️⃣ OLA 1984 is relevant to trespassers and it may be relevant here as arguably the client became a trespasser when she climbed onto the banister. When dealing with any claim which involves occupiers, it is important firstly to decide whether or not the person injured is a visitor, which will fall to be decided under the OLA 1957, or whether they are a non-visitor, which will fall to be decided under the OLA 1984. It is important to go through the relevant sections methodically. This case illustrates how someone entering premises can start as a visitor but by their behaviour become a trespasser, so both Acts must be considered. But here the candidate falls into the trap of thinking that due to the lack of warning signs, liability may attach under the OLA 1984: remember that warning signs about dangers which are obvious are not required.

5️⃣ The Defective Premises Act is not relevant as this relates to buildings that are defective in some way and it is the defect in the premises that has caused injury to the claimant. The staircase was not defective, and it is the client's actions of climbing on it that led to her injuries.

6️⃣ The *Geary* case is very similar to the client's claim, and it should therefore be noted that Geary was unsuccessful in her claim on the basis that the danger was so obvious that the defendants were not required to provide warnings or alter the access to the banister. In this scenario, it is again obvious that sliding down a banister is dangerous. The candidate has failed to appreciate that the facts of *Geary* are very similar to the client's situation, and as a consequence has missed an opportunity to manage the client's expectations.

7️⃣ The *James* case is not very relevant to the client's situation, and the candidate fails to reach the assessment criteria here. That case involved a guest at a hotel and an open window, and there was also much consideration as to whether a civil claim could be founded on the basis of a criminal prosecution under the health and safety legislation. Also, the reduction in damages does not set a precedent as it very much depends on the facts of the case and the claimant's contribution to the injury.

8️⃣ The client should not be encouraged to issue proceedings. Consideration should always be given to the practice direction on pre-action conduct and protocols.

Does this answer meet the threshold?

When assessing the second memo against the SQE2 legal research assessment criteria, it is unlikely that it would meet the threshold standard for SQE2 legal research. The candidate has misinterpreted the law and made assumptions about case law, which are incorrect. The answer was also too brief and does not show full understanding of how the facts of the case will affect the court's decision.

SQE2 can assess any of the areas on the SQE1 dispute resolution specification. Below is another example of how a different part of the specification could arise in the context of SQE2 legal research.

■ QUESTION 2

Email to candidate

From: Partner
Sent: 2 April 202#
To: Candidate
Subject: Patricia Royle – Holiday sickness claim

A new client, Patricia Royle, has contacted the firm to discuss a potential claim for her and her family following a holiday to Turkey. Patricia confirms that her wife and their three children (aged 11, 13 and 16) travelled from Manchester Airport to the five-star Hill Luxury Spa Hotel in Antalya, Turkey on 5 February for 14 nights. The holiday was booked through the package holiday company MOI Ltd and it was an 'all-inclusive' package costing £4,500, which included flights, transfers, accommodation, and all meals and drinks. The family had to pay for tours and trips separately.

Patricia maintains that the hotel itself was very nice but that the food hygiene was awful. She and her family developed a sickness bug two days into the holiday. Her two youngest children were hospitalised and had to be placed on drips. She says that the hospital took stool samples and they found salmonella bacteria in the samples. The whole family was prescribed a course of antibiotics.

Patricia is adamant that their illness was not due to heat, over-consumption, dehydration or external food. The family ate all their meals at the hotel apart from lunch at a local restaurant on the second day.

She also maintains that she witnessed one of the chefs handling meat, then raw vegetables, spaghetti and the bin while wearing the same pair of gloves, which he then wore to prepare the family's food. At that point, Patricia asked him to change his gloves but he simply took them off and put only one new glove back on. He reheated bolognaise in a frying pan and then used the same pan to cook a vegetable-based sauce. Patricia also said that birds randomly flew in and out of the restaurant as it was open air.

She said that the cooked rice was stored in big trays sat on bains-marie but without lids so the rice was just warm. None of the food was hot, and due to the amount of food on offer Patricia was of the view that it was all reheated but not to a high enough temperature to kill the germs. Furthermore, there was no supervision of the guests handling food in the self-service station so the potential for contamination was immense. She says that the hand gel stations were empty, with no one enforcing the use of hand gel.

Patricia complained to the hotel but they denied any wrongdoing and blamed the family's illness on sunstroke. The hotel had put on a pool party on the first day they arrived, and the family stayed by the outside pool all day. Later that evening, Patricia and her wife went to a cocktail party while the older daughter looked after the younger two children.

Patricia has also complained to MOI Ltd about the food poisoning, but they have stated that they cannot be held responsible for the hotel's food preparation.

Patricia would like to know whether she is able to bring a claim for holiday sickness against the hotel or the holiday company MOI Ltd. She wants to move quickly on this matter as she is considering moving abroad and wants to tie up any loose ends in this country before she goes.

Please research the answer to this question, using the sources provided, and report back to me so that I can prepare my advice to Patricia.

I would like you to include, for my reference, your legal reasoning, mentioning any key sources or authorities.

Many thanks

Partner

Note to candidates:

Given the time constraints of this assessment, we have not provided the full text of some primary sources. Where the full text of a primary source is not provided, candidates may nevertheless cite the primary source on the basis it is referred to in one or more of the secondary sources provided and the full text can be checked at a later date.

Information displayed is as obtained on date of search, for example purposes only. Information herein is not to be relied upon outside of the purposes of this sample question.

Attachments

You have been provided with the following sources listed alphabetically in order of source name. The order of presentation is not intended as a guide to the order in which they should be consulted.

PLEASE NOTE THAT PART OR ALL OF SOME OF THESE SOURCES MAY NOT BE RELEVANT TO ANSWERING THE QUESTION.
1. Consumer Rights Act 2015, c 15 ss 6–11, 49
2. MOI Ltd's online brochure (www.MOIHolidays.co.uk)
3. Package Travel and Linked Travel Arrangements Regulations 2018 (SI 2018/634) Regulation 15
4. Pre-Action Protocol for Resolution of Package Travel Claims
5. Supply of Goods and Services Act 1982, c 29 ss 4, 6–8, 13
6. *Wood and another v TUI Travel plc (trading as First Choice)* [2017] EWCA Civ 11.

* * *

Source 1

Contains public sector information licensed under the Open Government Licence v3.0.

Consumer Rights Act 2015, c 15 ss 6–11, 49

6 Contracts for the hire of goods

(1) A contract is for the hire of goods if under it the trader gives or agrees to give the consumer possession of the goods with the right to use them, subject to the terms of the contract, for a period determined in accordance with the contract.
(2) But a contract is not for the hire of goods if it is a hire-purchase agreement.

7 Hire-purchase agreements

(1) A contract is a hire-purchase agreement if it meets the two conditions set out below.

(2) The first condition is that under the contract goods are hired by the trader in return for periodical payments by the consumer (and 'hired' is to be read in accordance with section 6(1)).

(3) The second condition is that under the contract ownership of the goods will transfer to the consumer if the terms of the contract are complied with and—

    (a) the consumer exercises an option to buy the goods,

    (b) any party to the contract does an act specified in it, or

    (c) an event specified in the contract occurs.

(4) But a contract is not a hire-purchase agreement if it is a conditional sales contract.

What goods contracts are covered?

8 Contracts for transfer of goods

A contract to supply goods is a contract for transfer of goods if under it the trader transfers or agrees to transfer ownership of the goods to the consumer and—

(a) the consumer provides or agrees to provide consideration otherwise than by paying a price, or

(b) the contract is, for any other reason, not a sales contract or a hire-purchase agreement.

What statutory rights are there under a goods contract?

9 Goods to be of satisfactory quality

(1) Every contract to supply goods is to be treated as including a term that the quality of the goods is satisfactory.

(2) The quality of goods is satisfactory if they meet the standard that a reasonable person would consider satisfactory, taking account of—

    (a) any description of the goods,

    (b) the price or other consideration for the goods (if relevant), and

    (c) all the other relevant circumstances (see subsection (5)).

(3) The quality of goods includes their state and condition; and the following aspects (among others) are in appropriate cases aspects of the quality of goods—

    (a) fitness for all the purposes for which goods of that kind are usually supplied;

    (b) appearance and finish;

    (c) freedom from minor defects;

    (d) safety;

    (e) durability.

(4) The term mentioned in subsection (1) does not cover anything which makes the quality of the goods unsatisfactory—

    (a) which is specifically drawn to the consumer's attention before the contract is made,

    (b) where the consumer examines the goods before the contract is made, which that examination ought to reveal, or

    (c) in the case of a contract to supply goods by sample, which would have been apparent on a reasonable examination of the sample.

(5) The relevant circumstances mentioned in subsection (2)(c) include any public statement about the specific characteristics of the goods made by the trader, the producer or any representative of the trader or the producer.

(6) That includes, in particular, any public statement made in advertising or labelling.

(7) But a public statement is not a relevant circumstance for the purposes of subsection (2)(c) if the trader shows that—

    (a) when the contract was made, the trader was not, and could not reasonably have been, aware of the statement,

      (b) before the contract was made, the statement had been publicly withdrawn or, to the extent that it contained anything which was incorrect or misleading, it had been publicly corrected, or

      (c) the consumer's decision to contract for the goods could not have been influenced by the statement.

(8) In a contract to supply goods a term about the quality of the goods may be treated as included as a matter of custom.

(9) See section 19 for a consumer's rights if the trader is in breach of a term that this section requires to be treated as included in a contract.

10 Goods to be fit for particular purpose

(1) Subsection (3) applies to a contract to supply goods if before the contract is made the consumer makes known to the trader (expressly or by implication) any particular purpose for which the consumer is contracting for the goods.

(2) Subsection (3) also applies to a contract to supply goods if—

      (a) the goods were previously sold by a credit-broker to the trader,

      (b) in the case of a sales contract or contract for transfer of goods, the consideration or part of it is a sum payable by instalments, and

      (c) before the contract is made, the consumer makes known to the credit-broker (expressly or by implication) any particular purpose for which the consumer is contracting for the goods.

(3) The contract is to be treated as including a term that the goods are reasonably fit for that purpose, whether or not that is a purpose for which goods of that kind are usually supplied.

(4) Subsection (3) does not apply if the circumstances show that the consumer does not rely, or it is unreasonable for the consumer to rely, on the skill or judgement of the trader or credit-broker.

(5) In a contract to supply goods a term about the fitness of the goods for a particular purpose may be treated as included as a matter of custom.

(6) See section 19 for a consumer's rights if the trader is in breach of a term that this section requires to be treated as included in a contract.

11 Goods to be as described

(1) Every contract to supply goods by description is to be treated as including a term that the goods will match the description.

(2) If the supply is by sample as well as by description, it is not sufficient that the bulk of the goods matches the sample if the goods do not also match the description.

(3) A supply of goods is not prevented from being a supply by description just because—

      (a) the goods are exposed for supply, and

      (b) they are selected by the consumer.

(4) Any information that is provided by the trader about the goods and is information mentioned in paragraph (a) of Schedule 1 or 2 to the Consumer Contracts (Information, Cancellation and Additional Charges) Regulations 2013 (SI 2013/3134) (main characteristics of goods) is to be treated as included as a term of the contract.

(5) A change to any of that information, made before entering into the contract or later, is not effective unless expressly agreed between the consumer and the trader.

(6) See section 2(5) and (6) for the application of subsections (4) and (5) where goods are sold at public auction.

(7) See section 19 for a consumer's rights if the trader is in breach of a term that this section requires to be treated as included in a contract.

What statutory rights are there under a services contract?

49 Service to be performed with reasonable care and skill

(1) Every contract to supply a service is to be treated as including a term that the trader must perform the service with reasonable care and skill.

(2) See section 54 for a consumer's rights if the trader is in breach of a term that this section requires to be treated as included in a contract.

© Crown copyright

* * *

Source 2

MOI Ltd's online brochure (www.MOIHolidays.co.uk)

Our liability to our customers

MOI Ltd are the organisers of your travel package under the Package Travel and Linked Travel Arrangements Regulations 2018. MOI Ltd accept responsibility for ensuring the travel services you book with us are provided as described. Once you have commenced your holiday, and encounter any part of your travel arrangements that are not provided as promised due to the fault of our employees, agents, or suppliers, we will seek to compensate you appropriately, considering all relevant factors, including the cost of the holiday, the steps you took to minimise the inconvenience/damage suffered, and the extent to which the deficiency affected your enjoyment.

Personal injury, illness, or death

MOI Ltd are not liable for any injury, illness, or death, or consequent losses, suffered by you or any member of your party unless you can prove that such injury, illness, or death was caused by our negligence or that of our suppliers in performing our obligations under our contract with you. Compensation is conditional on you notifying us of any complaint and assigning to us any rights against any third party and your continued co-operation in connection with your claim.

Limitation of liability

MOI Ltd are not liable for any personal injury, death, or any type of loss resulting from activities not forming part of the package booked with us. We expect customers to report any incident immediately.

Our liability, except in cases involving death, injury, or illness, is limited to a maximum of three times the cost of your travel arrangements.

MOI Ltd's liability is limited by any relevant international conventions, such as the Montreal Convention (air travel), Athens Convention (sea travel), Berne Convention (rail travel), and Paris Convention (accommodation), which limit compensation for death, injury, delay, and loss or damage to baggage.

Applicable laws and regulations

The promises we make regarding the services we agree to provide or arrange as part of the contract, together with the laws and regulations of the country where your claim or complaint occurred, will be used to determine whether the services were properly provided. If the services complied with the local laws and regulations applicable at that time, they will be treated as properly provided, even if they did not comply with UK laws and regulations.

Additional in-resort services

Any additional in-resort services or products booked during your holiday do not form part of your package holiday. MOI Holidays does not accept any liability for any additional in-resort services or products provided by third party contractors.

Copies of travel service contractual terms

You can request copies of the travel service contractual terms or international conventions from our Customer Services Team at MOI Holidays, PO BOX 99, Manchester, M6 1DA. Under EU Regulation 261/2004 (or UK equivalent), you have rights to refunds and/or compensation from your airline in cases of denied boarding, cancellation, or delay to flights.

Unavoidable and extraordinary circumstances

If unavoidable and extraordinary circumstances prevent your scheduled return, we will cover the cost of necessary accommodation for a maximum of two nights.

Complaints and claims

If you have a complaint about any services included in your holiday or encounter a problem, including illness or injury, inform the relevant supplier (for example, hotelier, villa provider, cruise director), our local agent, representative, or Customer Operations team via the 24/7 Customer Helpline (0044 123 456 789) without undue delay. Complete a Customer Report Form (if available) while in resort.

If your complaint is not resolved locally, follow up within 28 days of returning home by writing to our Customer Service team at MOI Holidays, PO BOX 99, Manchester, M6 1DA, or your travel agent, providing your booking reference and all relevant information.

Illness or injury

If you fall ill or suffer an accident on holiday, consult a local doctor and visit your GP upon return. Should you wish to claim against us for an injury or illness, provide details of the local doctor you saw and your GP, along with written authority for us to obtain medical reports from both.

False or exaggerated claims will be reported to authorities, and we will seek to recover any payments made in connection with such claims, along with incurred costs.

Failure to follow these procedures may affect your rights under this booking.

*   *   *

Source 3

Contains public sector information licensed under the Open Government Licence v3.0.

Package Travel and Linked Travel Arrangements Regulations 2018 (SI 2018/634) Regulation 15

PART 4

Responsibility for the performance of the package

15. (1) The provisions of this regulation are implied as a term in every package travel contract.

(2) The organiser is liable to the traveller for the performance of the travel services included in the package travel contract, irrespective of whether those services are to be performed by the organiser or by other travel service providers.

(3) The traveller must inform the organiser without undue delay, taking into account the circumstances of the case, of any lack of conformity which the traveller perceives during the performance of a travel service included in the package travel contract.

(4) If any of the travel services are not performed in accordance with the package travel contract, the organiser must remedy the lack of conformity within a reasonable period set by the traveller unless that—

(a) is impossible; or

(b) entails disproportionate costs, taking into account the extent of the lack of conformity and the value of the travel services affected.

(5) Where the organiser does not remedy the lack of conformity within a reasonable period set by the traveller for a reason mentioned in sub-paragraph (a) or (b) of paragraph (4), regulation 16 applies.

(6) Where the organiser refuses to remedy the lack of conformity or where immediate remedy is required, the traveller—

(a) may remedy the lack of conformity; and

(b) is entitled to reimbursement of the necessary expenses.

(7) A traveller to whom paragraph (6)(a) applies is not required to—

(a) set a reasonable period pursuant to paragraph (4), and

(b) if such a period has been set, wait until the end of the period,

before the traveller remedies the lack of conformity.

(8) Where the organiser is unable to provide a significant proportion of the travel services as agreed in the package travel contract, the organiser must offer, at no extra cost to the traveller, suitable alternative arrangements of, where possible, equivalent or higher quality than those specified in the contract, for the continuation of the package, including where the traveller's return to the place of departure is agreed.

(9) Where the organiser offers proposed alternative arrangements which result in a package of lower quality than that specified in the package travel contract, the organiser must grant the traveller an appropriate price reduction.

(10) The traveller may reject the proposed alternative arrangements offered under paragraph (8) only if—

(a) they are not comparable to the arrangements which were agreed in the package travel contract; or

(b) the price reduction granted is inadequate.

(11) Where—

(a) a lack of conformity substantially affects the performance of the package; and

(b) the organiser fails to remedy the lack of conformity within the reasonable period, the traveller may terminate the package travel contract without paying a termination fee and, where appropriate, is entitled to a price reduction, or compensation for damages, or both, in accordance with regulation 16.

(12) If—

    (a) the organiser is unable to make alternative arrangements, or

    (b) the traveller rejects the proposed alternative arrangements in accordance with paragraph (10),

the traveller is, where appropriate, entitled to a price reduction, or compensation for damages, or both, in accordance with regulation 16 without terminating the package travel contract.

(13) If the package includes the carriage of passengers, the organiser must, in the cases referred to in paragraphs (11) and (12), also provide repatriation of the traveller with equivalent transport without undue delay and at no extra cost to the traveller.

(14) Where the organiser is unable to ensure the traveller's return as agreed in the package travel contract because of unavoidable and extraordinary circumstances, the organiser must bear the cost of necessary accommodation, if possible of equivalent category—

    (a) for a period not exceeding 3 nights per traveller; or

    (b) where a different period is specified in the Union passenger rights legislation applicable to the relevant means of transport for the traveller's return, for the period specified in that legislation.

(15) The limitation of costs referred to in paragraph (14) does not apply to persons with reduced mobility as defined in point (a) of Article 2 of Regulation (EC) No 1107/2006 of the European Parliament and of the Council, concerning the rights of disabled persons and persons with reduced mobility when travelling by air (1) and any person accompanying them, pregnant women and unaccompanied minors, as well as persons in need of specific medical assistance, provided that the organiser has been notified of their particular needs at least 48 hours before the start of the package.

(16) The organiser's liability under paragraph (14) may not be limited by reason of unavoidable and extraordinary circumstances if the relevant transport provider may not rely on such circumstances under the applicable Union passenger rights legislation.

* * *

Source 4

Pre-Action Protocol for Resolution of Package Travel Claims

Preamble

2.1 This Protocol describes the behaviour the court expects of the parties prior to the start of proceedings where a claimant claims damages valued at no more than £25,000 in a Package Travel claim. If, at any stage, the claimant values the claim at more than the upper limit of the fast track, the claimant should notify the defendant as soon as possible.

2.2 The Civil Procedure Rules enable the court to impose costs sanctions where either party fails to comply with this Protocol.

Aims

3.1 The aims of this Protocol are to—
   (1) encourage the exchange of early and full information about the claim;
   (2) encourage better and earlier pre-action investigation by all parties;
   (3) enable the parties to avoid litigation by agreeing settlement of the dispute before proceedings are commenced;
   (4) enable the parties to narrow the issues in dispute before proceedings are commenced; and
   (5) support the proportionate and efficient management of proceedings where litigation cannot be avoided.

Scope

4.1 This protocol applies where—
   (1) the claim arises from a gastric illness contracted during a package holiday;
   (2) no letter of claim has been sent to the defendant before 7th May 2018;
   (3) the claim includes damages in respect of personal injury;
   (4) the claimant values the claim at not more than £25,000 on a full liability basis including pecuniary loss but excluding interest ('the upper limit'), and
   (5) if proceedings were started the small claims track would not be the normal track for that claim.

* * *

Source 5

Contains public sector information licensed under the Open Government Licence v3.0.

Supply of Goods and Services Act 1982, c 29 ss 4, 6–8, 13

PART I SUPPLY OF GOODS

Contracts for the transfer of property in goods

...

4 Implied terms about quality or fitness

(1) Except as provided by this section and section 5 below and subject to the provisions of any other enactment, there is no implied condition or warranty about the quality or fitness for any particular purpose of goods supplied under a **[F2**relevant contract for the transfer of goods]**.
[F5 (2) Where, under such a contract, the transferor transfers the property in goods in the course of a business, there is an implied condition that the goods supplied under the contract are of satisfactory quality.
F5 (2A) For the purposes of this section and section 5 below, goods are of satisfactory quality if they meet the standard that a reasonable person would regard as satisfactory, taking account of any description of the goods, the price (if relevant) and all the other relevant circumstances.
F6 (2B)................................
F6 (2C)................................
F6 (2D)................................

(3) The condition implied by subsection (2) above does not extend to any matter making the quality of goods unsatisfactory—
   (a) which is specifically drawn to the transferee's attention before the contract is made,
   (b) where the transferee examines the goods before the contract is made, which that examination ought to reveal, or
   (c) where the property in the goods is transferred by reference to a sample, which would have been apparent on a reasonable examination of the sample.]
(4) Subsection (5) below applies where, under a [F2relevant contract for the transfer of goods], the transferor transfers the property in goods in the course of a business and the transferee, expressly or by implication, makes known—
   (a) to the transferor, or
   (b) where the consideration or part of the consideration for the transfer is a sum payable by instalments and the goods were previously sold by a credit-broker to the transferor, to that credit-broker,
   any particular purpose for which the goods are being acquired.
(5) In that case there is (subject to subsection (6) below) an implied condition that the goods supplied under the contract are reasonably fit for that purpose, whether or not that is a purpose for which such goods are commonly supplied.
(6) Subsection (5) above does not apply where the circumstances show that the transferee does not rely, or that it is unreasonable for him to rely, on the skill or judgement of the transferor or credit-broker.
(7) An implied condition or warranty about quality or fitness for a particular purpose may be annexed by usage to a [F2relevant contract for the transfer of goods].
(8) The preceding provisions of this section apply to a transfer by a person who in the course of a business is acting as agent for another as they apply to a transfer by a principal in the course of a business, except where that other is not transferring in the course of a business and either the transferee knows that fact or reasonable steps are taken to bring it to the transferee's notice before the contract concerned is made.
[F7 (9) ....]

Contracts for the hire of goods

6 The contracts concerned

(1) In this Act [F12in its application to England and Wales and Northern Ireland] a '[F13relevant contract for the hire of goods]' means a contract under which one person bails or agrees to bail goods to another by way of hire, other than [F14a hire-purchase agreement] [F15, and other than a contract to which Chapter 2 of Part 1 of the Consumer Rights Act 2015 applies.]
(2) F16...............................
(3) For the purposes of this Act [F12in its application to England and Wales and Northern Ireland] a contract is a [F13relevant contract for the hire of goods] whether or not services are also provided or to be provided under the contract, and F17... whatever is the nature of the consideration for the bailment or agreement to bail by way of hire.

7 Implied terms about right to transfer possession, etc.

(1) In a [F13relevant contract for the hire of goods] there is an implied condition on the part of the bailor that in the case of a bailment he has a right to transfer possession of the goods by way of hire for the period of the bailment and in the case of an agreement to bail he will have such a right at the time of the bailment.
(2) In a [F13relevant contract for the hire of goods] there is also an implied warranty that the bailee will enjoy quiet possession of the goods for the period of the bailment except so far as the possession may be disturbed by the owner or other

person entitled to the benefit of any charge or encumbrance disclosed or known to the bailee before the contract is made.

(3) The preceding provisions of this section do not affect the right of the bailor to repossess the goods under an express or implied term of the contract.

8 Implied terms where hire is by description

(1) This section applies where, under a **[F13**relevant contract for the hire of goods]**, the bailor bails or agrees to bail the goods by description.

(2) In such a case there is an implied condition that the goods will correspond with the description.

(3) If under the contract the bailor bails or agrees to bail the goods by reference to a sample as well as a description it is not sufficient that the bulk of the goods corresponds with the sample if the goods do not also correspond with the description.

(4) A contract is not prevented from falling within subsection (1) above by reason only that, being exposed for supply, the goods are selected by the bailee.

PART II SUPPLY OF SERVICES

...

13 Implied term about care and skill

In a **[F53**relevant contract for the supply of a service]** where the supplier is acting in the course of a business, there is an implied term that the supplier will carry out the service with reasonable care and skill.

© Crown copyright

* * *

Source 6

Wood and another v TUI Travel plc (trading as First Choice) [2017] EWCA Civ 11

1   The issue in this appeal is whether Mr and Mrs Wood can recover damages, pursuant to the implied condition in section 4(2) of the Supply of Goods and Services Act 1982 ('the 1982 Act'), for acute gastroenteritis suffered while staying at the Gran Bahia Principe Hotel in the Dominican Republic in 2011 on an all-inclusive holiday contracted with TUI Travel Plc trading as First Choice ('First Choice'). The implied condition provides that where property in goods is transferred pursuant to a contract in the course of business, the goods must be of 'satisfactory quality'. His Honour Judge Worster concluded that the supply of food and drink to Mr and Mrs Wood constituted the supply of goods for the purpose of the 1982 Act. He decided that their illness was caused by contaminated food or drink that they were given in the hotel. It was not of 'satisfactory quality' for the purposes of section 4(2) because it was contaminated. Mr Wood was awarded damages which included £16,500 for pain, suffering and loss of amenity and Mrs Wood £7,500. It is unnecessary to expand upon the detail of the medical problems they suffered as a result of the gastroenteritis but the levels of damages (which are not the subject of challenge) are sufficient to show that the consequences were serious and not transitory.

2   First Choice appeal against the finding of liability under the 1982 Act on the basis that the contract did not contemplate that property in the food and drink would be transferred to Mr and Mrs Wood. They suggest that the consumption of food and drink provided at the hotel involved no transfer of property in that food or drink.

27   In my opinion, in the absence of any express agreement to the contrary, when customers order a meal property in the meal transfers to them when it is served. The same is true of a drink served by the establishment. That is so whether the transaction has no other components, for example in a restaurant or café, or the transaction provides other services, the most usual being accommodation. It is unreal to suppose, for example, that the pizza placed in front of a customer remains the property of the hotel or restaurant any more than the content of a glass of wine or lemonade could do so after it was served to a customer. The fact that the food and drink may be laid out in a buffet to which customers help themselves can make no difference. When the customer helps himself to the meal or pours himself a drink property in the fare becomes that of the customer.

28   It follows that the conclusion reached by the judge was correct. The contract between First Choice and Mr and Mrs Wood was a contract both for the supply of services and the supply of goods. The food and drink supplied to Mr and Mrs Wood at the hotel in the Dominican Republic were goods in which it was agreed that property would be transferred. Those goods were not of satisfactory quality because the food in question was contaminated. Whether goods are of satisfactory quality is a question of fact but where food is contaminated with bacteria that causes severe illness it is difficult to imagine that it could be described as of satisfactory quality.

29   Underlying this appeal was a concern that package tour operators should not become the guarantor of the quality of food and drink the world over when it is provided as part of the holiday which they have contracted to provide. Mr Aldous spoke of First Choice being potentially liable for every upset stomach which occurred during one of their holidays and the term 'strict liability' was mentioned. That is not what the finding of the judge or the conclusion that he applied the correct legal approach dictates. The judge was satisfied on the evidence that Mr and Mrs Wood suffered illness as a result of the contamination of the food or drink they had consumed. Such illness can be caused by any number of other factors. Poor personal hygiene is an example but equally bugs can be picked up in the sea or a swimming pool. In a claim for damages of this sort, the claimant must prove that food or drink provided was the cause of their troubles and that the food was not 'satisfactory'. It is well-known that some people react adversely to new food or different water and develop upset stomachs. Neither would be unsatisfactory for the purposes of the 1982 Act. That is an accepted hazard of travel. Proving that an episode of this sort was caused by food which was unfit is far from easy. It would not be enough to invite a court to draw an inference from the fact that someone was sick. Contamination must be proved; and it might be difficult to prove that food (or drink) was not of satisfactory quality in this sense in the absence of evidence of others who had consumed the food being similarly afflicted. Additionally, other potential causes of the illness would have to be considered such as a vomiting virus.

31   In this case, the judge heard evidence not only from Mr and Mrs Wood but also from suitable experts in the light of the medical position recorded in the records Mr Wood's admissions to hospital in both the Dominican Republic and the United Kingdom. In my view he was correct to conclude the provision of contaminated food by the hotel amounted to a breach of the implied condition found in section 4(2) of the 1982 Act. In those circumstances it is unnecessary to consider Mr Weir's alternative argument based upon the common law. I would dismiss the appeal.

Lord Justice McFarlane

32   I agree.

Sir Brian Leveson, P

33 I also agree. In relation to the metaphysical arguments about property in and ownership of food taken from a buffet, there can be little doubt that once food has been taken onto the plate of the guest, it has been appropriated to him or her. It would not be open to the hotel or guesthouse to complain that the guest had taken too much. As for the removal of food to eat later, that might be a breach of an implied term that the guest is entitled only to take that which he or she wishes immediately to consume for the relevant meal but it could hardly be more than that.

© Crown copyright

* * *

■ YOUR TURN

Have a go at answering question 2, remembering the guidance on pages 20–21.
• Refer to the structured approach in the SRA's assessment criteria on page 21.
• Create a list of the most salient legal points raised by the question.
• Timings are important: you will need to prepare and write your answer in one hour.

SQE1 Functioning legal knowledge link
Remember from chapter 2 of **Revise SQE: Dispute Resolution** that the pre-action protocols must be adhered to. Even where there is no relevant pre-action protocol, the Practice Direction on Pre-Action Conduct and Protocols (PDPACP) dictates pre-action rules that the parties must adhere to, and non-compliance can result in a party being penalised by the court at a later stage in the proceedings.

EVALUATING YOUR ANSWER

When you have attempted question 2, mark it yourself against the SQE2 legal research assessment criteria. Do you think your attempt met the threshold standard?

Now compare your attempt with the following key legal points and two sample answers to question 2. A circled number indicates that commentary is provided for this part of the answer. The commentary explains whether or not the sample satisfies the assessment criteria, and accordingly likely to meet the threshold SQE2 standard.

➡Key legal points: Question 2

In this assessment, part, or all, of the following sources are relevant to the question:
1. Consumer Rights Act 2015, c 15 ss 8–11, 49
2. MOI Ltd's online brochure (www.MOIHolidays.co.uk)
3. Package Travel and Linked Travel Arrangements Regulations 2018 (SI 2018/634) Regulation 15
4. Pre-Action Protocol for Resolution of Package Travel Claims
5. Supply of Goods and Services Act 1982, c 29 ss 4, 13
6. *Wood and another v TUI Travel plc (trading as First Choice)* [2017] EWCA Civ 11.

The following sources are not relevant to the question:
1. Consumer Rights Act 2015, c 15 ss 6, 7
2. Supply of Goods and Services Act 1982, c 29 ss 6–7.

Key legal points:

- You need to identify that liability may exist under separate legislation. The case law and the Supply of Goods Act predate the later Package Travel and Linked Travel Arrangements Regulations 2018, but reference can be made to both, in order to illustrate that you understand the development of the law and that it may be possible to also pursue a potential defendant under different legislation. When litigating, you will need to plead all relevant causes of action and evidence the same. Pointing this out to the partner ensures that you are complying with the SQE2 assessment criteria in identifying and using relevant sources.
- Highlight the pre-action protocol to follow. The memo suggests that the client wants to move quickly. You need to ensure that they take into consideration the pre-action protocol and provide advice that is not only client-focused but addresses the client's problem. While it may be necessary to issue proceedings at some point, you need to manage the client's expectations and advise that the court expects all parties to follow the relevant protocol.
- Assess the evidence and what further information is required. You need to ensure that you apply the law correctly to the client's situation: analyse the limited information provided and advise what other evidence needs to be obtained in order to successfully bring a claim under the regulations. Like any personal injury claim, the foundation starts in the law of negligence and whether there is a duty, whether it has been breached and whether that breach has caused loss and damage. Holiday sickness claims can be difficult to prove: unless the client undergoes a medical test at the time of the bout of sickness, which attributes the sickness to a specific bacterial infection through food, the only way to prove on balance that the sickness was due to poor hotel hygiene is to document and evidence the hotel's shortcomings.

◼ SAMPLE ANSWER 1 TO QUESTION 2

On reviewing the memo and the client's instructions, I have researched the relevant legislation and consider that the client and her family may have a claim under the Package Travel Regulations 2018. Under Regulation 15(2) of Regulations a term is implied that the defendant would be liable for the performance of the travel services included in the package travel contract, irrespective of whether those services were performed by the organiser or by other travel service providers. This indicates that any potential claim can be brought against MOI as this company organised the package, and if proceedings are necessary they can be issued against their registered office in the UK without the need to issue on the hotel outside the jurisdiction. ❶

In order to successfully bring a claim under the package regulations, the claimant and those of her family affected must prove that food poisoning was caused by breach on the part of the hotel of the express and/or implied terms or warranties of the holiday contract. ❷

Further or alternatively, the client must show that the food poisoning was caused by the proprietors and/or managers of the hotel who were agents or suppliers within the meaning of MOI Ltd's standard terms and conditions and/or within the meaning of Regulation 15 of the Package Travel Regulations. In order to achieve a successful claim, the holiday company MOI must be proved to be negligent and/or have caused the failure of, or improper performance of, the holiday contract. They will be liable for those acts and omissions. ❸

Also, there was an implied term of the package holiday contract pursuant to s 13 of the Supply of Goods and Services Act 1982 and/or s 49 of the Consumer Rights Act 2015 that the defendant would exercise the reasonable care and skill of an experienced tour operator in the selection and monitoring of accommodation allocated to the claimant. ❹

The claimants would need to prove that the hotel services supplied to the claimant fell below a reasonable standard/that tables, chairs, cloths, cutlery and crockery were stained and dirty/that the food was supplied from a buffet that had containers of uncovered hot and cold food/that wild and stray animals were allowed to be present in the buffet and dining areas.

Both statutes (s 13 Supply of Goods and Services Act 1992 and s 49 Consumer Rights Act 2015) contain mirror provisions that contracts for services (the Consumer Rights Act 2015 applying specifically to consumers) should be carried out with reasonable care and skill.

The client would also need to show that there was failure to devise and/or implement any system of inspection, supervision or monitoring of the standards and services offered at the hotel, either with regard to the selection of the hotel as accommodation for the claimant or in respect of identifying and remedying the defects causing or permitting the claimant to be exposed to the foreseeable risk of illness and/or bodily injury by reason of the condition of the hotel. Here we can evidence using witness statements potentially that the hotel did not carry out their catering duties with reasonable care and skill. We should also ask the client whether they took any photos or videos of the food or restaurant. ⑤

The client booked the holiday here in the UK and will be able to pursue the holiday company in this country. I note the hotel offered 'all-inclusive' food and drink but the client's family did eat outside the hotel once, so we will need to show that their illness must have come from the hotel. If we can evidence the hygiene concerns at the hotel, the client has better chances of proving their illness was caused by the hotel. We will need medical evidence to support this. ⑥

Some tour operators expressly accept liability for personal injury caused by the negligence of their employees or agents, or undertake to ensure that all components of the holiday are provided to a reasonable standard. We would need to check, for example, the brochure or website from which the holiday was chosen, the booking confirmation and any tickets supplied for further terms and conditions. ⑦

The case of *Wood and another v TUI Travel plc T/A (trading as First Choice)* has similar case facts. It was held that consuming food at a hotel buffet was indeed the transfer of goods, thus enabling the claims to claim under the relevant legislation at the time (pursuant to s 4 of the Supply of Goods and Services Act 1982). However, this case predates the 2018 Regulations, so is helpful but the Consumer Rights Act 2015 strengthens the client's position. ⑧

I note the client wishes to move quickly, but the Pre-Action Protocol for Resolution of Package Travel Claims must be adhered to. I anticipate that we will need to obtain medical records for the client and her family, documentation appertaining to the booking of the holiday and photographs taken in the restaurant. ⑨

COMMENTARY

❶ The candidate introduces the most relevant legislation to illustrate that they have considered all the documentation and have been able to ascertain the most pertinent legislation. As the incident occurred outside the UK, it is important to consider where proceedings should be issued if this becomes necessary. The candidate has demonstrated their knowledge of this issue, showing that they understand the objective of the client and the meaning of the legislation.

❷ The candidate continues to apply the relevant facts to the legislation to highlight that they understand the issues.

❸ The candidate should ensure they point out the significance of the standard of skill and care expected by the defendant. This demonstrates that they are able to conduct legal research from a variety of sources and that they can apply the law comprehensively to the client's situation.

④ There were several pieces of legislation provided. Referring to the relevant legislation is essential and illustrates that the candidate is aware that a claim can be brought in the alternative under each relevant Act.

⑤ It is important to point out what evidence is required to prove the claim, referencing the necessary legislation. Highlighting that the laws mirror each other shows that the candidate has a deep grasp of the issue, and that consumer legislation seeks to protect the consumer, or in this case the traveller.

⑥ This demonstrates that the candidate can identify the legal principles which are relevant to the area of practice, and can apply them appropriately and effectively to individual cases.

⑦ Not all information is provided by the client, and noting this allows the candidate to demonstrate their understanding that there is further evidence to be ascertained.

⑧ The TUI case is provided to illustrate how the courts addressed the issues of the transfer of goods pursuant to the Supply of Goods and Services Act 1982. However, because it predates the 2018 Regulations, it was important for the candidate to point this out and illustrate their ability to apply the relevant legislation.

⑨ Even though the client may have the grounds of a successful claim, any pre-action protocols must be complied with so as not to fall foul of the CPR and the overriding objective. Again the candidate shows that they understand the bigger picture and the need to manage client expectations of a speedy resolution to this matter.

Does this answer meet the threshold?
The sample answer above contains all of the information that the client requires and that the candidate has been asked to provide. The candidate has selected relevant information about the legal issue and the client's problem from the sources provided, and their answer is therefore likely to meet the threshold standard for SQE2 legal research.

Now consider the second sample answer to question 2.

■ SAMPLE ANSWER 2 TO QUESTION 2

I have reviewed the above case and am of the view that the facts mirror those of the case of *Wood and another v TUI Travel plc (trading as First Choice)* [2017] EWCA Civ 11. In that case the claimants suffered food poisoning at a hotel buffet and the court held that the transfer of food was transfer of property for the purpose of the Supply of Goods and Services Act 1992. The facts of this case mirror those of our client's case. For this reason I am of the view that the client and her family can bring a claim. The client will need to prove that she and her family ate solely from the hotel, and the sticking point may be the odd occasion when the family ate away from the hotel. We will need to check where they ate and what was consumed. ①

It will be necessary to issue proceedings in a foreign jurisdiction and I will provide further details of the process once I receive your instructions. We will need to find out whether the hotel has a registered office in the resort where the client and her family stayed. I note that the client wants to move quickly so I suggest we issue proceedings as soon as possible. ②

We will need to gather documentary evidence to support the client's claim, in the form of witness statements and medical records. We will request the client to provide any documentation she has in relation to the booking of the holiday. If the client has retained photographs and videos of the hotel and the restaurant, this will be helpful to the claim. I suggest we draft these with a view to bringing the claim at the earliest convenience. We will need to provide medical evidence to support the client's claims. ❸

We can also pursue the holiday company under the Consumer Rights Act 2015 on the basis that the service provided by the hotel was substandard. Under the regulations the hotel must provide goods to a satisfactory standard. The Supply of Goods and Services Act also allows for a claim to be brought on the basis that the client expected the food at the hotel to be of a certain standard and that there was an implied duty of care and skill in the goods, ie the food transferred to the client and her family. ❹

The 2018 Regulations also support a claim being brought against the hotel. This is because the regulations specifically seek to protect holidaymakers abroad. ❺

There is a pre-action protocol but on the basis that the client has already complained to the hotel and they have refused to entertain her claim, we need not delay the issue of proceedings. We can plead the Consumer Rights Act, Supply of Goods and Services Act along with the 2018 Regulations. We will need to obtain medical evidence to support the claim however, so I suggest we request a copy of the client's medical records and instruct a medical expert as the next step. ❻

COMMENTARY

❶ The case cited has similar facts but predates the Package Travel and Linked Travel Arrangements Regulations 2018. From the details of the case cited, the appeal centred around whether the defendant travel company were in breach of implied conditions as to satisfactory quality of goods, and whether consumption of food and drink involved the transfer of property under the Supply of Goods and Services Act 1982, s 4(2). However, the candidate should have used the Package Travel and Linked Travel Arrangements Regulations 2018 as the starting point for any advice, as the legislation deals with the point specifically. The candidate also states the wrong year the Act was passed (1992 instead of 1982).

❷ The Package Travel and Linked Travel Arrangements Regulations 2018 allow the issue of proceedings against the travel company which is based in the UK, so there is no need to issue proceedings outside the UK's jurisdiction. Issuing proceedings in a foreign jurisdiction would therefore not be the legally correct action to take, so the candidate has failed to apply the law correctly here.

❸ As with most types of litigation, there are pre-action protocols to follow. Even if there were not a specific protocol, the issuing of proceedings prematurely is likely to result in penalties from the court. In this case, the Pre-Action Protocol for Resolution of Package Travel Claims applies. Source 4 should draw the candidate's attention to the need to ensure the overriding objective (to deal with cases justly and at proportionate cost) is born in mind. If the assessment deals with a claim involving potential litigation but does not present you with a relevant pre-action protocol, you must always reference the practice direction for pre-action conduct and protocols; this relates to the overriding objective and the need to engage in the early exchange of evidence, in an attempt to narrow the issues and accordingly use court time efficiently. The overriding objective means that there should be early exchange of evidence as this ensures the matter can be dealt with proportionately with 'a cards on the table' approach. Evidence gathering is therefore important.

❹ This is accurate but should be expanded upon. The candidate should highlight the specific sections of the legislation that are relevant, as the advice here is vague and would fall short of illustrating competency under the assessment criteria. The law should be applied correctly to the client's situation. There are therefore other sources which are also relevant here that the candidate has omitted. More details should be given regarding the gathering of evidence and how the court will assess the hotel's behaviour. Reference should be made to s 15(2) of the Package Travel Regulations 2018, namely that the holiday company is liable to the traveller for the performance of the travel services included in the package travel contract, irrespective of whether those services are to be performed by the organiser or by other travel service providers.

⑤ This is incorrect as the claim should be brought against the tour operator MOI, not the hotel.

⑥ The candidate should not advise the partner to incur the expense of a medical report without first gathering all the relevant evidence and initiating a claim adhering to the Pre-Action Protocol for Resolution of Package Travel Claims. The candidate is not applying the law correctly here, and in trying to speed things along they are neglecting the overriding objective. Remember that due to the pre-action protocols, litigation is often the last resort.

Does this answer meet the threshold?

When assessing the second memo against the SQE2 legal research assessment criteria, it is unlikely that it would meet the threshold standard for SQE2 legal research. The candidate has not applied the law correctly, has made inaccurate statements and has not complied with the relevant pre-action protocol.

■ KEY POINT CHECKLIST

This chapter has covered the following key knowledge points:
- The SQE2 assessment criteria for legal research and how to apply them in the context of dispute resolution in contract and tort.
- A suggested structure for approaching an SQE2 legal research question.
- Examples of researched answers that are either likely or unlikely to meet the threshold standard, with full commentary on their strengths and weaknesses.

■ SUMMARY AND REFLECTION

To succeed in the SQE2 legal research assessment, think carefully about the legal issues the question is presenting in relation to the sources provided. It is a good idea to sketch a short plan to structure your answer.

Bear in mind that the assessment criteria requires you to apply the law both correctly and comprehensively, so it is very important that you focus on the relevant documents provided. Also remember that some documents will not be relevant: you need to state this within your answer and explain why they are not relevant.

Make sure you practise legal research and writing legal advice based on research, in respect of contractual and tortious issues. As assessment time is limited, you need to be able to read the documents quickly and ascertain which are relevant and which are not. Remember to use professional language, as you are communicating with a partner who is requesting advice, which will form the basis of their letter to the client.

Now take the time to reflect and consider what you might still need to work on and whether you feel completely confident in your legal research skills in the context of dispute resolution.

3

Legal writing

■ MAKE SURE YOU KNOW

This chapter explores the skill of legal writing in the context of dispute resolution. Legal writing in this area is one of the legal skills that will be assessed on day one of the SQE2 assessments (see the Introduction for more detail). Remember that the SQE2 can test candidates' knowledge of not only the processes associated with dispute resolution, but also the application of contractual or tortious principles to those processes. Before attempting the questions in this chapter, boost your knowledge of the subject area by reviewing *Revise SQE: Dispute Resolution*, *Revise SQE: Tort Law* and *Revise SQE: Contract Law*. You will also see that some of the scenarios used in the practice examples contained in those texts are built on in this book, so you can see the ways in which the SQE2 skills assessment incorporates the legal principles you ought to have learned for your SQE1 examinations.

This chapter provides examples of how different options for dispute resolution, case management and the rules relating to disclosure could arise in the context of a legal writing SQE2 assessment.

■ SQE ASSESSMENT ADVICE

As you work through this chapter, remember to pay particular attention in your revision to:
- the inclusion of relevant facts in the sample answers
- the way in which letters and emails are structured, and how this could be applied generally
- the information you are given about clients/recipients in the sample assessments and how the advice is tailored to them
- the use of clear and concise language in the sample answers
- how the law is applied to the client's situation
- the way in which any ethical or professional conduct issues are identified and resolved.

See the Appendix for the SRA's performance indicators in legal writing.

■ INTRODUCTION TO LEGAL WRITING IN DISPUTE RESOLUTION

The SQE2 assessment usually includes scenarios which occur in day-to-day legal practice. A key aspect of practising in the field of dispute resolution is the ability to follow verbal advice given by a solicitor to a client with a clearly articulated written communication.

Your SQE2 assessment in legal writing will be based on reading a memo or email from a partner which asks you to provide advice to a client. This will usually follow a fictitious telephone call which has taken place between the partner and the client. The question will give you some direction about the areas you need to cover in your letter or email, but you will need to apply your knowledge of those areas to the scenario and communicate the relevant advice to the client clearly and concisely in writing. This chapter will provide examples of how you can do this and meet the criteria for SQE2 legal writing assessment at the same time.

The key to success in your SQE2 legal writing assessment is approaching the question in a structured manner. Try adopting the following method:

1. Once you have read the question, write down the key legal and procedural points that you feel need to be communicated to the client.
2. Use headings or subheadings based on key legal points to form the structure of the letter or email you are asked to write.
3. Write your answer.
4. Review your answer, keeping in mind the SQE2 legal writing assessment criteria.

Assessment technique

When reviewing your answer, read the draft and ask yourself whether or not it answers the client's question(s) clearly and concisely. Avoid using long sentences and overly technical language, and plan the structure of your letter or email based around what you have been asked to consider.

SQE2 legal writing assessment criteria

Try to remember these points as you construct your answer:

Skills

1. Include relevant facts.
2. Use a logical structure.
3. Advice/content should be client- and recipient-focused.
4. Use clear, precise, concise and acceptable language which is appropriate to the recipient.

Application of law

5. Apply the law correctly to the client's situation.
6. Apply the law comprehensively to the client's situation, identifying any ethical and professional conduct issues and exercising judgement to resolve them honestly and with integrity.

In chapter 1 of *Revise SQE: Dispute Resolution*, we considered the different options for dispute resolution and the pre-action steps which the Civil Procedure Rules (CPR) encourages parties to take prior to issuing proceedings. Question 1 demonstrates how your knowledge of this topic could be tested in the context and format of an SQE2 legal writing assessment.

■ QUESTION 1

Email to candidate

From: Partner
Sent: 2 April 202#
To: Candidate
Subject: Mr Oliver Brown (65 Westerham Villas, Birmingham, B4 3NY) – Dispute with James Fairley Limited

I am acting for Mr Oliver Brown in connection with a building dispute with James Fairley Limited ('JFL'). JFL were contracted by Mr Brown in October last year to build an orangery at the rear of his property. It was agreed that JFL would commence work on 1 February this year and complete the work by 31 March. Mr Brown paid a deposit of £5,000 to JFL, with the balance being due on completion of the work.

By the end of March, only the foundations had been built. No work had been commenced on the structure of the orangery itself. When Mr Brown raised this with JFL, they explained that the stormy weather of February had meant that they were unable to do the work they needed to during that month, but that they have been able to make significant progress during March. Mr Brown is, however, furious that the orangery is not ready on time and has asked us to 'sue JFL for as much as we can'. He informed me that his relationship with JFL is very poor following these discussions.

I explained to Mr Brown over the phone that there are certain pre-action steps that we should take prior to issuing proceedings, one of which is considering alternative methods of dispute resolution. I also advised him that arbitration would not be suitable in this claim and that he should therefore consider mediating a settlement with JFL, with which he agreed. He asked me whether there would be any consequences if he refused, but unfortunately his signal failed and we were cut off before I could explain what those would be. Mr Brown has now emailed me to ask if we could outline our advice to him in writing.

I would like you to write a letter to Mr Brown explaining the following:

1. **The steps that should be taken prior to issuing proceedings.**
2. **What mediation is, and its advantages and disadvantages as a method of settling his dispute with JFL.**

Mr Brown is not a lawyer, so it is important that your explanation is clear and simple. However, he is intelligent and astute, and will insist on understanding everything, so you will need to provide brief legal explanations where appropriate.

Thanks

Partner

Note to candidates:

You do not need to consider or deal with any issues concerned with limitation.

* * *

■ YOUR TURN

Have a go at answering question 1, remembering the guidance on pages 55–56.
- Refer to the structured approach in the SRA's assessment criteria on page 56.
- Create a list of the most salient legal points raised by the question.
- Timings are important: you will need to prepare and write your answer in 30 minutes.

SQE1 Functioning legal knowledge link
Remember from chapter 1 of **Revise SQE: Dispute Resolution** that parties are required to consider alternative methods of dispute resolution (ADR) before issuing proceedings, and that failing to do so could lead to adverse cost consequences being imposed on them. There are a number of potential methods of ADR, but the SQE2 assessment only requires you to consider two: arbitration and mediation.

EVALUATING YOUR ANSWER

When you have attempted question 1, mark it yourself against the SQE2 legal writing assessment criteria. Do you think your attempt met the threshold standard?

Now compare your attempt with the following key legal points and two sample answers to question 1. A circled number indicates that commentary is provided for this part of the answer. The commentary explains whether or not the sample satisfies the assessment criteria, and accordingly likely to meet the threshold SQE2 standard.

➡️Key legal points: Question 1

- Explore with the client alternative methods of dispute resolution before issuing proceedings – the existence and expectation of pre-action protocols/practice direction on pre-action conduct and their expectations in terms of being willing to engage in ADR before seeking the assistance of the court.
- Explain the advantages and disadvantages of mediation and arbitration – with application of the key advantages and disadvantages of both types of ADR to the client's scenario, such as cost, speed of resolution and flexibility.

■ SAMPLE ANSWER 1 TO QUESTION 1

[*The law firm's address and contact details*]

65 Westerham Villas
Birmingham
B4 3NY

2 April 202#

Dear Mr Brown

Re: Your dispute with James Fairley Limited

Thank you for consulting our firm in connection with the above dispute. For ease, I will refer to James Fairley Limited as 'JFL' throughout this letter. The purpose of this letter is to provide advice on the steps you are strongly encouraged to take prior to issuing proceedings, as well as setting out your options at this stage. ❶

Steps to be taken prior to issuing proceedings ❷

You mentioned during the course of our telephone conversation that you were keen to proceed with legal action against JFL. However, prior to instigating a claim through the court, the rules which govern civil procedure in England and Wales set out a series of steps which ought to be taken by parties who wish to pursue legal action against another. In this case, we are required to follow the guidance set out in the Practice Direction for Pre-Action Conduct and Protocols ('the Practice Direction'). The relevant steps contained within the Practice Direction are set out in this paragraph.

First, we are required to write to JFL detailing the claim we are bringing against them. This letter will include the basis on which the claim is made, a summary of the facts and a breakdown of the financial compensation we are seeking from them. We will also enclose any documents which are relevant to the dispute within the letter.

Second, the Practice Direction strongly encourages parties to consider using alternative methods of dispute resolution to attempt to reach a settlement with their opposing party. In this case, it would involve using a non-court-based method of dispute resolution to try to reach an agreed settlement with JFL. The two most common methods of alternative dispute resolution are arbitration and mediation. I advised you over the telephone that arbitration would not be suitable for this dispute and you agreed. I have therefore set out for you the benefits and disadvantages of attempting mediation in the next section of this letter. Provided you were happy in principle to attempt to mediate a settlement, we would include an offer to mediate in the initial letter to JFL.

Mediation and its advantages and disadvantages ❸

Mediation involves settlement by agreement between the parties, with discussions and negotiations facilitated by a mediator. Once parties to a dispute have consented to mediate in principle, they will nominate and agree on the appointment of an independent mediator. Following this, both parties will send written position statements to the mediator which set out a background to the case, the points in dispute and any proposals they may have for settlement. The mediator will use this document to prepare for the face-to-face meeting.

A date and place for the mediation will then be agreed between the parties and the mediator. On the day, you will occupy a separate room from JFL, and the mediator will 'shuttle' between them. It is the mediator's job to break down the dispute and direct the parties towards a personalised settlement which is to the satisfaction of both parties.

There are numerous advantages to mediation, but I am going to focus on the ones which are most relevant to your case. First, if a settlement can be mediated at an early stage then your overall legal costs associated with the dispute will be significantly lower than if the matter were to proceed to court and then, ultimately, trial. Second, a mediation session can also be arranged reasonably quickly and can result in swifter resolution of the dispute compared with litigation. Third, mediated settlements have the advantage of being more flexible. For example, you might be prepared to extend the timescale for JFL completing the work but negotiate a reduction in the overall price of the work to account for the delay. A mediated settlement would give you the flexibility to do this. Finally, if an agreement is reached and signed, this is enforceable by the court in the event JFL were to renege on any part of the settlement.

The primary disadvantage I can foresee with mediating this dispute is the state of the relationship between you and JFL. If there is no willingness on either side to negotiate, mediation can sometimes prove a futile exercise as it is reliant on the parties wanting to settle, even if they do not have a clear picture of what the terms of such a settlement could look like prior to the mediation taking place. There is also nothing to stop a party from leaving a mediation part way through. This would mean that the costs of the mediation would be wasted, leaving you essentially in the same position in relation to the action as you are now.

I hope that the information contained in this letter is helpful and I look forward to receiving your further instructions.

Yours sincerely

Partner

COMMENTARY

① The introductory paragraph sets out the purpose of the letter. If you consider this from the perspective of a non-legally trained client, it explains why the candidate is writing to them and what information they will be able to learn from reading your letter. Also note the abbreviation of James Fairley Limited to 'JFL'. This is an example of using clear and precise language for the client, and would also save time in the assessment from having to type the lengthy name of the defendant repeatedly!

② Note how this section begins by explicitly referring to the information the client provided over the telephone. This lets the examiner know that the candidate is using the information they have been given about the client, which is one of the assessment criteria. The text then draws the client's attention to the existence of pre-action requirements, but crucially does not list or detail every one of these. It focuses on the points most relevant to the client's claim as well as implicitly tackling the client's desire to refer this matter to the court straight away. We are also told in the assessment brief that the client is intelligent and astute, and that he will insist on understanding everything. The letter therefore refers to the rules and Practice Direction which strongly encourage the use of alternative methods of dispute resolution. The end of this section introduces the next. This then provides a natural platform to discuss the advantages and disadvantages of mediation, which is one of the assessment's express requirements.

③ This section begins by explaining what mediation is and how it works in language appropriate to the client. This is, again, to ensure that the client understands everything about the process and how it works so that he can make an informed decision on how to proceed. Note here that the content is selective. For example, in the section detailing mediation, the example only focuses on the advantages which are most applicable to the client's situation. It does not cover, for instance, the fact that mediating disputes is a good way of preserving an ongoing business relationship, as this would not be something which would be especially relevant to the client's ultimate goals. The letter also uses an example of how mediation could result in a more flexible solution being reached in the client's particular situation than that which could be achievable through court. It adopts a similar approach to the disadvantages, using the information given about the state of the relationship between the client and JFL to explain how mediation may not work in this particular circumstance. This is a good technique to show the examiner that the candidate understands the client's situation and is applying the relevant law or principles to that situation.

Does this answer meet the threshold?

The sample answer above contains all of the information that the client requires and that the candidate has been asked to provide. It is therefore likely to meet the threshold standard for SQE2 legal writing assessment. The answer contains all aspects of the assessment criteria for legal writing and, where appropriate, the examiner is directed specifically to the areas of the letter which deal with those criteria. It is important to remember that this is an assessment after all: let your examiners know that you are familiar with the criteria by which you are being assessed!

Now consider the second sample answer to question 1.

■ SAMPLE ANSWER 2 TO QUESTION 1

[The law firm's address and contact details]

65 Westerham Villas
Birmingham
B4 3NY

2 April 202#

Dear Mr Brown

Re: Your dispute

I understand that you have been in contact with our firm regarding a dispute you currently have. I am writing to you to give you some advice. ❶

First, you need to write to JFL and explain that you have a claim against them. This will allow you both to understand each other's position, make decisions about how to proceed, try to settle the issues without proceedings, consider a form of alternative dispute resolution (ADR) to assist with settlement, support the efficient management of those proceedings and reduce the costs of resolving the dispute. ❷

If this does not work, you must proceed to trying to settle the matter through mediation. Mediation is a process where parties meet to discuss the dispute between them to try to reach a negotiated settlement. There are many advantages to mediation, including the fact that it is cheaper than court and you can preserve a business relationship with the opposing party as it is less adversarial. If you do reach a settlement, this can be detailed in an agreement which both parties sign and is then binding. Sometimes, this agreement will also be sent to court if proceedings have already been issued by that point. It is also open to parties who do not reach an agreement to come back to mediation later down the line. The courts will penalise you for failing to mediate with the other side, as they expect you to do this under the relevant pre-action protocol. ❸

I hope that the information contained in this letter is helpful and I look forward to receiving your further instructions.

Yours sincerely

Partner

COMMENTARY

❶ The letter opens poorly. The first paragraph does not specify what the dispute concerns, what advice is going to be provided or why the candidate is writing to the client.

❷ The letter then goes on to state that the client needs to write to JFL, but offers no explanation as to why this is and makes no reference to the Practice Direction for Pre-Action Conduct and Protocols, save for copying and pasting the objectives of pre-action conduct straight from the Practice Direction itself. It makes no attempt to explain any of the legal terms used to the client.

The way the letter is drafted suggests that the client is responsible for writing to and negotiating with JFL. It is clear from the memo that the client has instructed the firm to assist the client with the dispute, therefore it would be much more appropriate to state that the firm will engage in this pre-action conduct on the client's behalf and in accordance with their instructions.

❸ The opening sentence of the third paragraph is problematic, as it incorrectly states that the client is obliged to proceed to mediation, which is not the case. Under the Practice Direction, parties are required to consider alternative forms of dispute resolution, which can be evidenced in the form of a written offer to mediate. However, ultimately the client will choose whether they wish to pursue alternative methods of dispute resolution, or run the risk of being penalised with costs sanctions if they do not. While the letter then references the advantages of mediation, it does not make any attempt to tailor these to the client's particular situation. For example, the preservation of a business relationship is simply not relevant here. Finally, the letter mentions penalties for failing to mediate, which again is incorrect. Penalties exist for parties failing to consider mediation, which is something entirely different. Therefore, this paragraph would not meet the SQE2 assessment requirements of being legally correct and legally comprehensive.

The letter also does not inform the client what the penalties are, and it finishes by referring to a pre-action protocol but offers no explanation about what this is or why it is relevant. The candidate uses technical terms which are not appropriate to the recipient, thereby failing to meet an assessment requirement of SQE2 legal writing.

Does this answer meet the threshold?

When assessing the second letter against the SQE2 legal writing assessment criteria, it is unlikely that this letter would meet the threshold standard for SQE2 legal writing. Sections of the legal analysis are incorrect, and the content does not fully provide the information the candidate has been asked to detail.

The SQE2 assessment can assess any of the areas on the SQE1 dispute resolution specification. Another example of how a different part of the specification could arise in the context of legal writing on SQE2 is given in the following question.

■ QUESTION 2

Email to candidate

From: Partner
Sent: 14 November 202#
To: Candidate
Subject: Grace Records Limited (12 The Market, Newcastle upon Tyne, NE1 5RN) – Dispute with Francis Stern

I am acting for Grace Records Limited ('GRL') in connection with a dispute with one of their customers, Francis Stern. GRL's business involves selling vinyl records to customers globally. They are based in Newcastle. Mr Stern, who resides in Liverpool, contacted GRL via their website in February 202# seeking to purchase the entire back catalogue of Bruce Springsteen on vinyl. GRL responded and agreed to source and supply the records for Mr Stern. In March of that year, the parties agreed by email a price of £875.00 for the supply and postage of the vinyl records. GRL sourced the records and sent them to Mr Stern in April, along with an invoice requesting that payment be made within 28 days. Mr Stern paid the balance of the invoice immediately upon receipt.

GRL closed during October 202# to allow the owners to spend a month in the USA on holiday, specifically so that they could visit Sun Studio in Memphis, TN. When they returned to the shop on 1 November, they found an envelope enclosing a judgment in default ordering them to pay Mr Stern the sum of £875.00. They also found an N1 claim form, which had been delivered separately, which alleged that the vinyl collection they had sold to Mr Stern was not fit for purpose and that he was therefore claiming full recovery of the value of the vinyls from GRL. GRL strongly deny this, as they had all of the records independently tested prior to sending them to Mr Stern which revealed no problems.

I would like you to write GRL a letter explaining the following:

1.   **What a judgment in default is, and the reasons why such an order may have been made against GRL.**
2.   **What GRL would need to show in order to successfully apply to set aside the judgment in default.**

The owners of GRL are not lawyers, so it is important that your explanation is clear and simple. However, they are intelligent and astute, and will insist on understanding everything, so you will need to provide brief legal explanations where appropriate.

Thanks

Partner

*   *   *

■ YOUR TURN

Have a go at answering question 2, remembering the guidance on pages 55–56.
- Refer to the structured approach in the SRA's assessment criteria on page 56.
- Create a list of the most salient legal points raised by the question.
- Timings are important: you will need to prepare and write your answer in 30 minutes.

SQE1 Functioning legal knowledge link

Remember from chapter 4 of **Revise SQE: Dispute Resolution** that judgment in default arises from a failure to respond to a claim form and particulars of the claim being served on a party within either 14 days (for acknowledgement of service) or 28 days (for defence). Without this context, *comprehensively* explaining the concept of judgment in default to a lay client will be very difficult.

EVALUATING YOUR ANSWER

When you have attempted question 2, mark it yourself against the SQE2 legal writing assessment criteria. Do you think your attempt met the threshold standard?

Now compare your attempt with the following key legal points and two sample answers to question 2. A circled number indicates that commentary is provided for this part of the answer. The commentary explains whether or not the sample satisfies the assessment criteria, and accordingly likely to meet the threshold SQE2 standard.

➡Key legal points: Question 2

- Judgment in default – explain how it can be applied for and when a claimant can apply for it (either after 14 days since the date of service if the defendant fails to file acknowledgement of service or after 28 days since the date of service if the defendant fails to file a defence to the action). Note the fact that, as it currently stands, the client is liable for the full amount claimed as judgment has been entered against him.
- How to set aside judgment in default – describe the procedure involved and what the client needs to show the court. Discuss both mandatory and discretionary ground and advise that discretionary is the only one which can apply here. Suggest evidence which the client can use to prove the fact that he was out of the country

when the claim form and particulars of claim were served. Ensure that the need to apply promptly is highlighted.
• Status of the claim in the event that an application to set aside default judgment was successful – explain that parties will essentially revert to the position they were in before judgment in default was granted, ie that the client will need to submit a defence.

■ SAMPLE ANSWER 1 TO QUESTION 2

[The law firm's address and contact details]

Grace Records Limited
12 The Market
Newcastle upon Tyne
NE1 5RN

2 April 202#

Dear Sirs

Re: Your dispute with Francis Stern

Thank you for instructing our firm in connection with your dispute with Francis Stern. My supervising partner has summarised the situation and asked me to write to you with some advice. The purpose of this letter is to provide you with general information about what a judgment in default is and why it has been made against you, and what you would need to show in order to make a successful application to set aside the judgment. ❶

What is judgment in default?

When somebody wishes to make a claim, such as Mr Stern in this case, they need to complete a claim form and particulars of claim. These documents are sent to the court and, most commonly, the court will then serve, or send, them to the defending party by first-class post. In this case, the defendant is you.

Once a claim form and particulars of claim have been served on a defendant, they are required to respond by either completing an acknowledgement of service or sending a defence to the court within 14 days of service. If the defendant chooses to acknowledge service within the 14 days, they are then allowed up to 28 days after initial service of the claim form to file their defence. If the defendant does not take either of these steps, the claimant is then entitled to apply for judgment in default, which is the term for judgment being awarded in the claimant's favour on the basis that the defendant has failed to respond to the claim form being served on them within the relevant timescales.

In this case, as you were on holiday at the time the claim form and particulars of claim were served, you were not able to respond to them within the relevant timescales, enabling Mr Stern to make an application for judgment in default. This technically means that, as things currently stand, you are legally obliged to pay Mr Stern the full amount claimed. However, there are steps you can take at this point to try to have the judgment set aside, which if successful would mean that the judgment would be declared invalid, allowing you to defend the claim that Mr Stern has made against you. This is covered in the next paragraph. ❷

What do you need to show to successfully set aside judgment in default?

The Civil Procedure Rules set out two grounds on which you can base an application to set aside judgment in default. The first is that the defendant has either filed their acknowledgement of service or defence on time or that they settled and paid the claim before the judgment in default was entered. In this case, neither of those circumstances apply so we would not be able to apply on this ground. The second ground is that the defendant shows to the court that they have a real prospect of successfully defending the claim, or that there is some other good reason why you should be allowed to defend the claim.

Based on what you told my supervising partner, we could make an application on the second ground, based on both elements. To show that you have a real prospect of successfully defending the claim, we could rely on any evidence you have from your independent assessor showing that there were no problems with the vinyl collection prior to sale to Mr Stern. Please supply us with copies of any evidence you have from your independent assessor. To show that there is some other good reason as to why you should be allowed to defend the claim, we can argue that you were on holiday at the time the claim form and particulars of the claim were served and that you therefore could not respond to them within the relevant timescales. Please therefore provide us with copies of your flight tickets and accommodation receipts to prove that you were out of the country on the relevant dates.

The final requirement is that the application is made promptly. We would therefore need to move swiftly with making this application, if you wished us to do so on your behalf.

It is the court's decision on whether to set aside the judgment in default, but if we were successful in the application this would mean that the original judgment would be declared invalid and you would be allowed to proceed to defending the claim. It is also important to note at this point that, even if you are successful in setting aside the judgment, this is not indicative of whether you would successfully be able to defend proceedings at trial. Success in our application would merely mean that the court recognises that you have a valid defence which can be used in a full trial of the issues. ❸

I hope that the information contained in this letter is helpful. I look forward to receiving your further instructions as soon as possible, along with copies of the evidence requested.

Yours sincerely

Partner

COMMENTARY

❶ As with sample answer 1 to question 1, it is good practice to inform the client at the beginning of the letter about its purpose and what information they can glean from it.

❷ The second section begins by explaining to the client how the process for making a claim works and, most importantly, how and by when the defendant needs to respond in order to defend it. Without this background context, the client would not be able to clearly determine exactly why a judgment has been made against them. Note how the letter sets out the parties' individual obligations and then personalises them, applying the requirements specifically to the client's situation and explaining to them gently what they failed to do rather than adopting a more accusatory tone. The letter also covers the client's current position regarding liability to remind them of the consequences of failing to make an application to set aside judgment at this point. Clear, succinct and accurate language is used throughout, and the paragraph is both legally correct and comprehensive, given the extent of its application of the law to the client's situation.

❸ Again, this section commences by setting out the relevant law, but quickly proceeds to explaining which ground is most applicable to the client's case and why. This ensures a logical structure is followed, an assessment requirement of SQE2 legal writing. It also refers specifically to the documentary evidence the client will need to supply to support the application, directing them clearly on their next steps if they wish to proceed. This is good practice as it ensures that the client is aware of what they need to do following receipt of the letter and it demonstrates further the application of the law to the client's situation, another of the assessment requirements. The letter goes on to explain the concept of promptness, and why it is so important in this context, and to explain the discretionary nature of the application without using any complex legal terminology. Finally, the letter reminds the client that success in this application does not indicate that the defence will ultimately be successful. This demonstrates a comprehensive understanding of the law and how it applies to the client's specific situation, as well as managing the client's expectations as to the significance of the outcome.

Does this answer meet the threshold?

The sample answer above contains all of the information that the client requires and that the candidate has been asked to provide. It communicates the information clearly and focuses on the client: instead of explaining the process in the abstract, it repeatedly shows how the advice relates directly to the client's situation. It is therefore likely to meet the threshold standard for SQE2 legal writing.

Now consider the second sample answer to question 2.

■ SAMPLE ANSWER 2 TO QUESTION 2

[The law firm's address and contact details]

Grace Records Limited
12 The Market
Newcastle upon Tyne
NE1 5RN

2 April 202#

Dear Sirs

Re: Your dispute with Francis Stern

I have been asked to write to you about the dispute you have ongoing with a person called Frances Stern and I understand that you want some advice about it. ❶

Judgment in default is where a defendant has failed to acknowledge service or defend a claim within 14 days or 28 days depending on which they choose to do, so the reason you have had judgment in default entered against you is because you have not responded to a claim made by the claimants. However in this case you were on holiday and could not respond to the claim so we would plan on using one of the grounds in CPR 13 to apply to set aside the default judgment against you. The grounds are (1) the defendant has either filed their acknowledgement of service or defence on time, or that they settled and paid the claim before the judgment in default was entered; (2) the defendant shows to the court that they have a real prospect of successfully defending the claim, or that there is some other good reason why you should be allowed to defend the claim. We could assist you with making this application.

If we are successful then this would mean that you could defend the claim, but if we lose then you will have to pay the claimant the full amount claimed. However as the ground we will be using is discretionary, there is no guarantee that we will be successful as we must persuade the court that you were on holiday and could not respond to the claim. ❷

Yours sincerely

Partner

COMMENTARY

1 The introduction here is badly written and vague, and the language is too informal. This would not be regarded as acceptable language suitable for the recipient and does not meet the assessment criteria.

2 This section makes no attempt to explain to the client exactly what judgment in default is, how it can arise and, perhaps most importantly, the legal consequences of the client currently having a judgment entered against them. It uses terminology such as 'judgment in default', 'set aside', 'discretionary' and 'CPR 13' without giving the client any explanation on what those terms mean and their significance; this therefore means that the letter would not be regarded as recipient-/client-focused, which is one of the assessment requirements for SQE2 legal writing. Even though the letter mentions the specific grounds of an application to set aside judgment in default, it does not make any attempt to apply these to the client's situation. It simply says that the client was on holiday and can therefore apply to set the judgment aside. The letter also fails to mention the evidence which is necessary to support the application, which would be expected. Finally, there is no mention of the need for promptness, a requirement under the CPR, so the letter is therefore not legally comprehensive.

Does this answer meet the threshold?

When assessing the second letter against the SQE2 legal writing assessment criteria, it is unlikely that this letter would meet the threshold standard for SQE2 legal writing. The information provided is significantly lacking in detail and the candidate makes no real attempt to apply the law to the client's scenario.

■ KEY POINT CHECKLIST

This chapter has covered the following key knowledge points:
- The SQE2 assessment criteria for legal writing and how to apply them in the context of dispute resolution in contract and tort.
- A suggested structure for approaching an SQE2 legal writing question.
- Examples of written answers which are both likely and unlikely to meet the threshold standard, with full commentary on their strengths and weaknesses.

■ SUMMARY AND REFLECTION

To meet the threshold standard in the SQE2 legal writing assessment, take your time to read the question properly, think about the legal points the question is asking of you and sketch out a short plan to follow for the structure of your letter.

Remember that the SQE2 assessment requires you to apply the law both correctly *and* comprehensively. It is really important to consider the relevant law and explain how it is applicable to the wider context of the client's scenario as well as to the more obvious narrow points.

Make sure you practise writing letters in client-friendly language; using too much legal jargon or legalistic terms without an accompanying explanation means that your letter will not be clear to the client recipient, and you will be penalised for this in the assessment.

Now take the time to reflect and consider what you might still need to work on, and whether you feel completely confident in your legal writing skills in the context of dispute resolution.

4

Legal drafting

■ MAKE SURE YOU KNOW

This chapter investigates the skill of legal drafting in the context of dispute resolution. Day one of the SQE2 assessments will include two exams in dispute resolution, and legal drafting is one of the legal skills that may be tested (see the Introduction for more detail). As well as being assessed on the legal principles of dispute resolution, you will also be tested on the practices associated with this area of the law. We strongly recommend that you read this revision guide and attempt the questions only when you are familiar with the contents of *Revise SQE: Dispute Resolution*, *Revise SQE: Tort Law* and *Revise SQE: Contract Law*.

This chapter provides examples of how different scenarios relating to dispute resolution could arise in the context of a legal drafting SQE2 assessment.

■ SQE ASSESSMENT ADVICE

As you work through this chapter, remember to pay particular attention in your revision to:
• using clear, precise, concise and acceptable language
• structuring the document appropriately and logically
• drafting a document which is legally correct
• drafting a document which is legally comprehensive; make sure you can identify ethical and professional conduct issues, and exercise your judgement to resolve them honestly and with integrity.

See the Appendix for the SRA's performance indicators in legal drafting.

■ INTRODUCTION TO LEGAL DRAFTING IN DISPUTE RESOLUTION

The SQE2 assessment will be based on scenarios which typically occur in legal practice. A key aspect of practising in the field of dispute resolution is the ability to draft legal pleadings if you enter litigation in respect of your client's claim. The SQE2 assessment in legal drafting will be based around a case study with accompanying documents, and you will be asked to draft pleadings, ensuring that the document is legally correct and pleads your client's case in a comprehensive and logical manner. This chapter will provide examples of how you can do this and meet the assessment criteria for SQE2 legal drafting.

We recommend that you approach your SQE2 legal drafting assessment in a structured manner. Try adopting the following approach:
1. Once you have read all the documentation, write down the key facts, legal issues and cause of action which are relevant to the matter.
2. Draw up a plan to structure your drafting around those key facts and legal issues.
3. Complete your legal drafting.
4. Review your answer, keeping in mind the SQE2 legal drafting assessment criteria.

Assessment technique

When reviewing your answer, check you have dealt with each relevant fact/legal issue and correct cause of action, cross-referencing the relevant information presented in the documents. This prevents you from omitting important information. Remember that when drafting legal documents, you must use clear, succinct and plain language to make the point with clarity.

SQE2 legal drafting assessment criteria

Try to remember these points as you construct your answer:

Skills

1. Use clear, precise, concise and acceptable language.
2. Structure the document appropriately and logically.

Application of law

3. Draft a document which is legally correct.
4. Draft a document which is legally comprehensive, identifying any ethical and professional conduct issues and exercising judgement to resolve them honestly and with integrity.

In chapters 1 and 2 of **Revise SQE: Tort Law**, we considered duty of care, breach of duty and causation in relation to the law of negligence. Question 1 demonstrates how your knowledge of this topic could be tested in the context of a road traffic accident and personal injury claim in the SQE2 legal drafting assessment.

■ QUESTION 1

Email to candidate

From: Partner
Sent: 3 December 202#
To: Candidate
Subject: Alyssa Bham – RTA 1 April 202#

You will recall that we submitted the client's claim for personal injury following her road traffic accident through the MOJ Portal and the third party disputed liability. The matter has exited the portal and we have notified the third party and their solicitors via a letter of claim that we intend to commence proceedings.

The third party, Mr Sean Hardwicke, insists that he is not to blame for the accident; he says that our client was indicating to turn right and flashed her lights to indicate to him that he should join the carriageway. You will note our client strongly denies this and we are instructed to commence proceedings. The third party has instructed solicitors, Clintons LLP.

The client wishes to claim for lost earnings, physiotherapy costs, policy excess and the cake she had collected on the day of the accident (Attachment 1 is her draft witness statement). There is no need to include a claim for the vehicle loss as her insurers have dealt with this and will await the outcome of the claim before pursuing the third-party insurers. We will need to send the medical report of Mr Khan dated 1 August 202# with the claim.

Please draft the particulars of claim using the template provided (Attachment 2). Some fields have been pre-populated by our case management system. You should include a claim for statutory interest pursuant to s 69 County Courts Act 1984 at the rate of 8% per year (to be calculated on conclusion of the claim). Alyssa Bham will sign the statement of truth.

I intend to send the claim form to the Civil National Business Centre for issue with the particulars of claim once you have drafted them.

Thanks

Partner

Attachment 1

Draft witness statement

I, Mrs Alyssa Bham of 75 Fleet Close, Prestwich, Westby, M12 2LT, will say as follows:

1. I am a qualified ophthalmologist working at the Westby Eye Clinic. I have been qualified for 15 years and worked at the Westby Eye Clinic for the last year. My date of birth is 28.12.86. My national insurance number is NA278342W.
2. On 1st April 202#, at about 3 PM, I was driving my Mini Cooper registration number LC23 SYD along the A55, Boston Road, approaching Westby city centre. I was driving very carefully as I had a birthday cake in the car with me which I had just collected from a local baker. The weather conditions were good, the road was straight and open and I had a clear view of the road.
3. I was just coming to the end of the dual carriageway section of the A55 and was travelling in the nearside lane at around 35 miles per hour. The road was clear ahead. As I approached the end of the carriageway and the junction with Prestwich Road, I slowed down, intending to turn left onto Prestwich Road. Just prior to the junction with Prestwich Road is Bamber Avenue on the left.
4. As I approached Bamber Avenue on the left all of sudden a car turned from Bamber Avenue onto the A55 into the path of my vehicle. I immediately reacted by braking sharply and swerving into the offside lane but the other vehicle continued to proceed onto the A55 and collided with the front nearside of my vehicle. This caused my vehicle to spin and hit the central reservation. The airbags on my car deployed. My car came to a rest in the central reservation.
5. I was conscious after the accident, but feeling very shocked and tearful. My neck, back and right knee were also giving me a lot of pain and I was afraid to get out of the car. I was told by a woman who had stopped that she had called the emergency services to the scene. This woman encouraged me to stay in the car until the emergency services arrived.
6. The emergency services arrived and I was helped out of the car and into an ambulance. The police took my name and address, whether I owned the vehicle and the speed at which I had been travelling. The police officer also spoke to the other driver, a male whom I now know to be called Sean Hardwicke. He was driving a black Land Rover Freelander registration number HC15 MAC.
7. The other driver told the police that I was indicating to move into the right hand lane and that I had flashed my lights indicating for him to join the carriageway. This is completely untrue. I was travelling home from collecting my daughter's birthday cake and I was in the nearside lane intending to turn left at the end of the A55. I saw his vehicle approaching the end of Bamber Avenue at speed and he failed to look before he proceeded onto the A55.
8. I was in terrible pain and was taken immediately by ambulance to Westby General Hospital where I stayed overnight. I continued to attend the hospital for physiotherapy for a period of eight weeks which helped ease my symptoms.

9. My solicitors arranged for me to see a consultant orthopaedic surgeon Mr Zaman Khan. I wish to rely upon the medical report of Mr Khan dated 1 August 202# in support of my claim. Mr Khan confirmed I sustained soft tissue injuries to my neck, back and right knee. He confirmed that my symptoms would recover fully within 12 months of the accident and recommended a further course of intense physiotherapy which I undertook from 5 September for eight weeks until 5 November. I paid for this privately and wish to claim for eight sessions which cost £100 per session.

10. I was absent from work for three months but as I had only been working at the Westby Eye Clinic for four months at the time of the accident, I was not entitled to sick pay. I lost three months' wages amounting to £9,000 net pay.

11. My car was written off after the accident and as I was fully comprehensively insured my insurers have paid me for the loss of the car. However, I wish to claim my policy excess of £350.

12. I also wish to claim for my daughter's birthday cake which was destroyed in the accident. The cake cost £175.

Signed

Date

Attachment 2

Particular of Claims Template

Claim No.

IN THE [insert name of court]

BETWEEN

[insert]   **Claimant**

and

[insert]   **Defendant**

PARTICULARS OF CLAIM

STATEMENT OF TRUTH

[I believe][The (Claimant or as may be) believes] that the facts stated in these particulars of claim are true. I understand that proceedings for contempt of court may be brought against anyone who makes, or causes to be made, a false statement in a document verified by a statement of truth without an honest belief in its truth.

I am duly authorised by the Claimant to sign this Statement

Signed: ....

Full name:

Office or Position Held:

Date: ....

The Claimant's Solicitors are Falcon & Co of Harrod Street, Prestwich, Westby M2 3GT where they will accept service of proceedings on behalf of the Claimant.

■ YOUR TURN

Have a go at answering question 1, remembering the guidance on pages 68–69.
- Refer to the structured approach in the SRA's assessment criteria on page 69.
- Create a list of the most salient legal points raised by the question.
- Timings are important: you will need to prepare and write your answer in 45 minutes.

SQE1 Functioning legal knowledge link

Remember from chapters 1 and 2 of **Revise SQE: Tort Law** that in order to bring a claim for negligence, you need to prove duty of care, breach of duty, and factual and legal causation.

EVALUATING YOUR ANSWER

When you have attempted question 1, mark it yourself against the SQE2 legal drafting assessment criteria. Do you think your attempt met the threshold standard?

Now compare your attempt with the following key legal points and two sample answers to question 1. A circled number indicates that commentary is provided for this part of the answer. The commentary explains whether or not the sample satisfies the assessment criteria, and accordingly likely to meet the threshold SQE2 standard.

➡️Key legal points: Question 1

These include the contents covered in CPR 16.4 as follows:
1. Set out a concise statement of the facts on which the claimant relies in a clear and logical manner to include:
   - the parties involved in the accident
   - the nature and details of the accident (in accordance with the written instructions)
   - allegations of breach of duty
   - particulars of injury, loss and damage
   - reliance upon medical evidence
   - details of interest claimed.
2. Use instructions to complete the heading and the statement of truth.

■ SAMPLE ANSWER 1 TO QUESTION 1

Claim No.

IN THE

Civil National Business Centre

BETWEEN

Alyssa Bham   **Claimant**

and

Sean Hardwicke   **Defendant**

PARTICULARS OF CLAIM

1. On 1 April 202#, the Claimant was driving her Mini Cooper registration number LC23 SYD along the A55, Boston Road, towards Westby when a collision occurred with a Land Rover Freelander motor car registration number HC15 MAC being driven by the Defendant. ❶
2. The Claimant's vehicle was proceeding in the nearside lane with the intention of turning left at the end of the A55. The Defendant's vehicle failed to give way to the Claimant's correctly proceeding vehicle and exited Bamber Avenue onto the A55 and into a collision with the nearside front of the Claimant's correctly proceeding vehicle. ❷
3. The entrance of traffic from Bamber Avenue onto the A55 Boston Road was controlled by a 'Give Way' sign and road markings. ❸
4. The collision was caused by the negligence of the Defendant. ❹

PARTICULARS OF NEGLIGENCE

The Defendant was negligent in that he:
   a. failed to keep a proper look out;
   b. failed to give way to the Claimant's vehicle;
   c. failed to see the Claimant's vehicle in time or at all;
   d. drove into the path of the Claimant's correctly proceeding vehicle;
   e. failed by means of the brakes, steering, gears or otherwise so to manage and control the motor car as to avoid the collision. ❺

5. As a result of these events the Claimant, who was born on 28 December 1986, has suffered pain, injury, loss and damage. ❻

PARTICULARS OF INJURY

The Claimant sustained a soft tissue injury to her neck, back and knee. She was taken to Westby General Hospital where she was treated as an inpatient for one day. Full particulars are contained in the report of Mr Zaman Khan (Orthopaedic Surgeon) dated 1 August 202# and annexed to these particulars. ❼

PARTICULARS OF SPECIAL DAMAGE

The Claimant seeks the following: ❽

Loss of earnings
The Claimant was absent from work from 1 April 202# to 1 July 202#

3 months at £3,000 net per month   £9,000

Physiotherapy charges
The Claimant underwent physiotherapy treatment from 5 September to
5 November 202#

8 weeks at £100 per session   £800

Policy excess
The Claimant's car was a total loss and the Claimant incurred
a policy excess   £350

Damaged items
The Claimant had collected her daughter's birthday cake prior to the accident
and the cake was destroyed in the collision   £175

6. In respect of damages awarded to her the Claimant is entitled to interest
    pursuant to section 69 of the County Courts Act 1984 at such rates and for such
    periods as seems just to the Court. ⑨

AND THE CLAIMANT CLAIMS: –
(1) Damages
(2) Costs
(3) Interest at the rate of 8% pursuant to section 69 of the County Courts Act 1984. ⑩

STATEMENT OF TRUTH

I believe that the facts stated in these particulars of claim are true. I understand that
proceedings for contempt of court may be brought against anyone who makes, or
causes to be made, a false statement in a document verified by a statement of truth
without an honest belief in its truth. ⑪
Signed: ....

Full name: Alyssa Bham

Date: 8 December 202#

The Claimant's Solicitors are Falcon & Co of Harrod Street, Prestwich, Westby M2
3GT where they will accept service of proceedings on behalf of the Claimant.

COMMENTARY

❶ The details of the vehicles and the parties driving those vehicles need to be set
out from the start, as this provides a clear understanding and introduction to the claim.

❷ The second paragraph sets out what each parties' role in the accident was, the
direction of travel and the actual location of the accident. Again this is required as
you are creating a setting in which you can plead your client's claim. Remember to
use clear and succinct language as per the assessment specification. It is advisable to
use plain terms and short sentences to ensure the document is drafted concisely.

❸ Reference is made to the priority of traffic so as to draw the court's attention to the
fact that the defendant failed to give way to the traffic on the A55, which in itself
illustrates that the defendant was driving below the standard of a reasonable
road user.

❹ It is important to state that the collision was caused by the defendant and then go
on to detail the specifics of negligence. The assessment criteria for the written skills
refer to clear, precise, concise and acceptable language. This may include using an
acceptable style of communication for the situation and recipient. Here the recipient is
the court and the defendant, so it is important to use formal language when drafting
this document.

(5) The particulars of negligence are quite standard when dealing with road traffic accidents. There is an established duty of care in respect of road users and the pleadings require particulars of that breach of duty to be itemised. Remember that ultimately failing to plead details could affect the outcome at trial. In demonstrating that the candidate has reached the standard of competency of a day one solicitor, they will need to demonstrate that they can apply fundamental legal principles in a way that addresses the client's needs and concerns.

(6) Having pleaded the specific details of the breach of the established duty of care between road users, the next element to be proved in a claim in negligence is that the breach of duty caused loss and damage. This is a logical structure, addressing one of the assessment criteria.

(7) Here details of the loss and damage (pain suffering and loss of amenity) can be proved by reliance on the medical report.

(8) Again just as the particulars of negligence are itemised, the particulars of the loss and damage (in this case special damages) are also itemised briefly. A separate schedule of special damages can be attached to the particulars of claim, but where special damages are limited it is acceptable to include them within the particulars of claim document.

Note that there is no spellcheck facility in the SRA's assessments, but you will not lose marks for spelling or grammatical mistakes that do not impact on the legal accuracy, clarity and/or certainty of the written text. You will also not be penalised for poor formatting, because of the limitations of the assessment software and the time constraints of the exam.

(9) When pleading interest it is important to note that interest needs to be pleaded using the correct Act. In this scenario, it is the County Court 1984 as the claim proceeds in the County Court. Interest on litigated claims can be a difficult area to understand. There are different rules in respect of the date interest starts to accrue, the rate that can be claimed and on what head of loss. Interest on general damages runs at 2% from the date of the service of the claim until such time as the claim settles (either at trial or due to a negotiated agreement) on all claims for personal injury and death that exceed £200. Generally, interest on special damages runs at half the 'appropriate rate' from the date of the accident until the date of trial or if the real part of the loss occurred on an identifiable date at the full 'appropriate rate' from that date until the date of trial. The 'appropriate rate' is the special account rate. At the time of writing the special account rate stands at 6%. The special account rate is set by the Lord Chancellor and can change in line with changes to the Bank of England base rate. Remember that interest also accrues on judgment debts. If the claim proceeds and the claimant is successful, the court will order the defendant to pay damages including interest and costs. If the defendant does not comply with the order and pay the amount, the claimant is entitled to interest on that judgment debt at a rate of 8% per year. The assessment criteria for legal drafting requires the document to be legally effective. Failing to mention interest or pleading an incorrect Act would have the potential consequence of rendering the claim for interest unfeasible and disadvantaging the client.

(10) The partner has asked that interest be pleaded at 8% but ultimately the court will decide what interest rate they award on the heads of claim as interest is always at the discretion of the court. Also remember in this scenario the claim is for an unspecified sum, and as such the candidate is unable to plead an actual figure as the court will assess the value of the claim at trial.

(11) The particulars of claim must be verified by a statement of truth pursuant to the Civil Procedure Rules (CPR) 22.1(1). The claimant or their legal representative can sign the statement of truth. If the claimant signs the statement of truth, the wording must be amended to 'I believe that the facts stated in these particulars of claim are true'. CPR 22.2(2) states that failure to verify a statement of case (the particulars of claim in this scenario) may lead to the court striking out the statement of case. As the partner has indicated that the claimant will sign the statement of truth, this has been correctly amended.

Does this answer meet the threshold?

The sample answer contains all of the information that the client requires and that the candidate has been asked to provide. The particulars of claim (accompanied by the claim form) could be sent to the court and thereafter issued and served on the defendant or their representatives. This answer is therefore likely to meet the threshold standard for SQE2 legal writing.

Now consider the second sample answer to question 1.

■ SAMPLE ANSWER 2 TO QUESTION 1

Claim No.

IN THE

County Court ❶

BETWEEN

A Bham   **Claimant**

and

S Hardwicke ❷   **Defendant**

PARTICULARS OF CLAIM

On 1 April 202#, the Defendant crashed into the Claimant on the A55, Boston Road, when the Defendant drove out of Bamber Lane into the Claimant. ❸

The Claimant was driving a Mini Cooper registration number LC23 SYD and the Defendant was driving a Land Rover Freelander motor car registration number HC15 MAC.

PARTICULARS OF NEGLIGENCE

The Defendant should have given way to the Claimant as they were entering a dual carriageway. ❹
a.   The Defendant caused the accident by failing to give way to the Claimant's vehicle;
b.   And not allowing the Claimant to proceed
c.   And failing to stop at the junction. ❺

PARTICULARS OF INJURY

Due to the accident the Claimant has suffered pain, injury, loss and damage. The Claimant relies on the report of Mr Zaman Khan (Orthopaedic Surgeon) dated 1 August 202#. ❻

PARTICULARS OF SPECIAL DAMAGE

The Claimant claims: ❼	
Lost earnings. She was off work for 3 months at £3,000 net per month	£9,000
Physio – 8 weeks at £100 per session	£800
Policy excess	£350
Cake destroyed	£175
Total	£10325
Interest @ 8%	£826 ❽

STATEMENT OF TRUTH

The Claimant believes that the facts stated in these particulars of claim are true. I understand that proceedings for contempt of court may be brought against anyone who makes, or causes to be made, a false statement in a document verified by a statement of truth without an honest belief in its truth. **9**
Signed: ....

Full name: Alyssa Bham

Date: 8 December 202#

The Claimant's Solicitors are Falcon & Co of Harrod Street, Prestwich, Westby M2 3GT where they will accept service of proceedings on behalf of the Claimant.

COMMENTARY

1 The particulars of claim should state the Civil National Business Centre as this is the central location of the issue of claims. Details of which County Court the claimant wishes the matter to be transferred to will be included on the N1 claim form which accompanies the particulars of claim.

2 The parties' full names should be included in the particulars of claim (PD7A, para 4.1). This is important as the case will be known by the names of the parties. If judgment is entered for the claimant against the defendant, the court judgment will be registered against the full name of the defendant. This answer would fail to fulfil the assessment specification as the document may not be legally effective. The court may struggle to register a County Court judgment against the defendant due to the lack of detail.

3 There is not enough detail here (and the candidate has called the road by the wrong name: Bamber Lane instead of Bamber Avenue). The particulars of claim should contain a concise statement of facts on which the claimant relies (CPR 16.4(1) (a)). The particulars should explain who the parties are and brief details of the accident so that the court can understand the issues. It is good practice to number the paragraphs in the particulars of claim for ease of reference when the court is being heard at trial. This answer section does not fulfil the assessment criteria as the document may not be legally effective.

4 The sentence is awkward and should be rephrased. The pleading needs to set out clearly what it is that the defendant failed to do that they should have done, and/or what the defendant did that they should not have done. When drafting particulars of claim, the claimant should identify the issues in dispute between the parties in sufficient detail so that the defendant can understand the case pleaded against them. The particulars of claim should enable the defendant to know the case they have to meet which ensures that the parties can properly prepare for trial. Remember that in order to fulfil the assessment the candidate must use clear, succinct and accurate language.

5 Here the details are lacking. In drafting the particulars of negligence, the claimant should view the exercise as an audit, ensuring the cause of action is sufficiently set out so as to include each element where the defendant's actions or omissions fell below the standard of care. This part of the document highlights specifically the breach of duty (see chapters 1 and 2, *Revise SQE: Tort Law*).

6 Here the particulars fail to comply with CPR PD 16, paras 4.1–4.4. The particulars must include the claimant's date of birth and brief details of the claimant's personal injury. As the claimant is relying upon the evidence of a medical practitioner, the medical report should also be attached to the particulars of claim (and referred to as such). Again this may render the document not legally effective as per the assessment criteria.

7 As the claim is for personal injury, the claimant must attach to her particulars of claim a schedule of details of any past and future expenses and losses which she claims. It is good practice to attach a separate schedule of losses if there are more than a few heads of claim.

⑧ As losses are limited to four items, it is acceptable to list the losses in the body of the particulars of claim. However, the losses need to be itemised in more detail so that the defendant knows the case they have to answer in respect of quantum.

⑨ The statement of truth is incorrect. If the claimant is signing the statement of truth it should read 'I believe that the facts stated in these particulars of claim are true', as specified in paragraph 2.1 of Practice Direction 22 of the CPR. An incorrect statement of truth may render the document legally ineffective as per the assessment criteria.

Does this answer meet the threshold?

When assessing the second particulars of claim against the SQE2 legal drafting assessment criteria, it is unlikely that these particulars of claim would meet the threshold standard for SQE2 legal drafting. There is a lack of accurate and succinct information, and the possibility that the document may not be legally effective.

Below is another example of how a different part of the SRA specification could arise in the context of legal drafting in an SQE2 assessment.

■ QUESTION 2

Email to candidate

From: Partner
Sent: 10 June 202#
To: Candidate
Subject: Flower Club Ltd – contract claim

I have recently taken instructions from Emily Jenkins, the sole director of Flower Club Ltd regarding a litigated breach of contract claim (Attachment 1). Emily creates and installs floral displays using dried flowers and pampas grass. She recently took a commission to create displays for Hanah Ahmed who was hosting her daughter's 21st birthday party. Emily tells me that the claimant contacted her via her website and placed an order for four floral displays and a floral arch to be created, delivered and installed on 31 March 202# for the party. Emily has provided us with a copy of the invoice (Attachment 2) (she was paid the day before the event in full). I have also spoken to Emily on the telephone today and she advises the following regarding the allegations in the particulars of claim:

The client took the order via the website and upon receipt she emailed the claimant to advise that due to supply issues she may not be able to create four pampas clouds but that she had enough product to create three clouds. The client advises that the clouds take a few hours each to create and each one requires in the region of 100 stems. The client cannot object to points 1 and 2 in the particulars of claim but she takes issue with the claim that she has breached the Consumer Rights Act.

In respect of the displays, they were all the correct colour – black and white. Emily had agreed to arrive at 9 AM but there was a serious accident on the M6 (well documented as it made the news headlines) involving multiple vehicles, and she called the claimant as soon as the traffic stopped, to advise her of the delay. The claimant was understanding but disappointed as could be expected, and she even sent a text message stating that this was not a problem and that the client should drive carefully.

In respect of the description and quality of the products, the client has produced more than 50 of the pampas clouds and 20 pampas and dried flower arches from the date she set up her business to the date she created the displays for the claimant's party and has since created the same amount, and she has never encountered this issue with the transfer of dye. In response to paragraph 6 of the particulars of claim, the client says that she told the claimant when she arrived and realised there was underfloor heating that this could affect the products used in the displays. The client says that the claimant was dismissive of her advice to turn the underfloor heating off to preserve the quality of the products, as she thought her guests would get cold.

The client also always draws customers' attention to the small print on her invoice that states that the displays are made from natural products and that they are affected by different environments.

The client states that she worked tirelessly to install the displays and that she told the claimant that due to supply issues which she had mentioned in her previous email, she only had enough to create three large pampas clouds or two large and two small pampas clouds, and that she gave the client the option to choose once she arrived at her house. The client says that the claimant took a long time to make a decision as she was dealing with caterers, and that this is the reason that she did not finish the clouds until the guests arrived. Also the client maintains that throughout the event there were several influencers live streaming and uploading video clips to their social media. The first few videos/streams show the venue and focus on the floral displays which are intact and for at least the first few hours of the party. There are then a few videos where the claimant's guests look a little drunk and one of them falls into the floral arch, grabs the display and brings it to the floor. The client advises that you can see the guests then treading parts of the dried flowers into the carpet. The client maintains that the videos show everything intact until the point where the guest destroys the floral arch.

The client did state that she has never had any complaints from customers prior to the event (she had been operating the business just three months when she was commissioned by the claimant). She has stopped using the black dye product due to this complaint.

In respect of the losses claimed, the client disputes she should reimburse the claimant any money at all. She maintains the only reason the products damaged the claimant's upholstery and carpets was due to the claimant insisting on having the underfloor heating on, that she had warned her about the display reacting as a natural product and that her guests ultimately caused the damage.

Please draft a defence to the particulars on the basis of the information provided, using the template form in Attachment 3. Emily will sign the statement of truth on behalf of the company.

Thanks

Partner

Attachment 1

Claim No. MC202424A

IN THE WESTBY
COUNTY COURT

BETWEEN

Hanah Ahmed   **Claimant**

and

Flower Club Ltd   **Defendant**

PARTICULARS OF CLAIM

1. At all material times:
    a) The Claimant was the purchaser of a number of pampas flower installations.
    b) The Defendant was and is a floral design company which specialised in the creation of floral displays using dried flowers and pampas grass.
2. On or about 1 February 202# the parties entered into a part written, part oral agreement ('the Agreement'). A series of emails which the Claimant will state forms part of the contract are attached to this particulars of claim. The agreement follows: That the Defendant create and supply four pampas 'clouds' and one pampas and dried flower arrangement arch to be delivered and installed on 31 March at the Claimant's property and that the Claimant do pay the Defendant £6,500 upon creation, delivery and installation of said items.
3. The following were express terms of the Agreement:
    a) The displays were to be made up of black and white dried flowers in accordance with the theme of the party the Claimant was hosting at her property; and
    b) The Defendant was to arrive at 9 AM on 31 March to install the displays with a view to ensuring the property was ready for the Claimant to host her party at 6 PM.
4. Further, the following terms were implied into the Agreement by the Consumer Rights Act 2015 ('the Implied Terms'):
    a) Section 9 (2) that the quality of the goods would meet a standard that a reasonable person would consider satisfactory. The quality of goods is satisfactory if they meet the standard that a reasonable person would consider satisfactory, taking account of—
        (i)   any description of the goods,
        (ii) the price or other consideration for the goods (if relevant), and
        (iii) all the other relevant circumstances (see subsection (5)); and
    b) Section 9 (3) that the quality of goods includes their state and condition; and the following aspects (among others) are in appropriate cases aspects of the quality of goods—
        (i)   fitness for all the purposes for which goods of that kind are usually supplied;
        (ii) appearance and finish;
        (iii) freedom from minor defects;
        (iv) safety;
        (v)   durability; and
    c) Section 10(3) that the goods were reasonably fit for purpose, the Claimant having made the Defendant aware of the particular purpose for which the Claimant required the goods, namely a floral display for an event; and
    d) Section 11(1) that the goods as described on the Defendant's website matched their description; and
    e) Section 49(1) that the contract to supply a service included a term that the Defendant must perform the service with reasonable care and skill.
5. Pursuant to the terms of the Agreement the Claimant paid the Defendant £6,500 for the creation, delivery and installation of the floral displays.
6. The Defendant has breached the terms of the Agreement as follows:

PARTICULARS OF BREACH OF CONTRACT

a) The Defendant arrived at the Claimant's property at 11.30 AM, two and a half hours late for the installation of the displays; and

b) The Defendant proceeded to install three pampas cloud displays, not four as ordered stating that there was an issue with one of the company's suppliers and that the Defendant did not have enough product to create a fourth pampas cloud; and

c) The Defendant created a pampas and dried flower arch using substandard pampas grass and dried flowers such that throughout the duration of the day and prior to the event the products disintegrated and the arch became unmanageable and had to be dismantled; and

d) The black pampas grass and dried flowers which fell from the floral arch were walked underfoot by party guests. The dye used to create the black products transferred from the product to the carpets and upholstery in the Claimant's house causing staining on the carpet and sofas; and

e) The Defendant was requested to complete the installation by 6 PM but failed to do so and was putting finishing touches to the pampas clouds as the guests arrived at 7 PM.

7. As a result of the Defendant's breach of the Agreement the Claimant has sustained loss and damage as follows:

PARTICULARS OF LOSS AND DAMAGE

7.1 Original amounts paid for creation, delivery and installation of floral displays	£6,500
7.2 Professional cleaning of sofas and upholstery	£750
7.3 Replacement carpet (main room)	£3,000
TOTAL	£10,250

8. The Claimant claims interest on any sums found to be due to the Claimant pursuant to section 69 of the County Courts Act 1984 at 8% or at such rate and for such period as the Court thinks fit.

AND the Claimant claims
(1) Damages for breach of contract
(2) Damages for stress and inconvenience
(3) Interest as set out above

STATEMENT OF TRUTH

I believe that the facts stated in this Particulars of Claim are true. I understand that proceedings for contempt of court may be brought against anyone who makes, or causes to be made, a false statement in a document verified by a statement of truth without an honest belief in its truth.

Full name: Hanah Ahmed

Name of Claimant's legal representative's firm: Conifer LLP

Signature: *Conifer LLP*

Date: 3 June 202#

Documents in these proceedings may be served on the Claimant at the following address: Conifer LLP, 1 High Street, Lytham St Annes, Lancashire FY8 1DA

Attachment 2

Flower Club Ltd

Let us create a beautiful space for the human race

INVOICE

To: Hanah Ahmed
17 The Grove
Lytham St Annes
Lancashire FY8 2PL

Flower Club Ltd will provide the following on 31 March 202#:

4 pampas clouds @£1000 each	**£4,000**
1 pampas and dried flower arch	**£1,250**
Delivery	**£250**
Installation	**£1,000**
Total	**£6,500**

Registered Office: Flower Club Ltd, Bank Chambers, Marton Industrial Estate, Lancashire FY3 3RT

Please note: all our products are natural and certain environments may have adverse effects on the product.

Attachment 3

Claim No. MC202424A

IN THE WESTBY
COUNTY COURT

BETWEEN

Hanah Ahmed   **Claimant**

and

Flower Club Ltd   **Defendant**

DEFENCE

STATEMENT OF TRUTH

I believe / The Defendant believes that the facts stated in this Particulars of Claim are true. I understand that proceedings for contempt of court may be brought against anyone who makes, or causes to be made, a false statement in a document verified by a statement of truth without an honest belief in its truth.

Full name:

Name of Defendant's legal representative's firm: Hoopers LLP

Signature: *Hoopers LLP*

Date:

Documents in these proceedings may be served on the Defendant at the following address: Hoopers LLP, 10 Pier Street, Lytham St Annes, Lancashire FY8 5TQ

* * *

■ YOUR TURN

Have a go at answering question 2, remembering the guidance on pages 68–69.
- Refer to the structured approach in the SRA's assessment criteria on page 69.
- Create a list of the most salient legal points raised by the question.
- Timings are important: you will need to prepare and write your answer in 45 minutes.

SQE1 Functioning legal knowledge link
Remember that when responding to the particulars of claim and drafting the defence, you must have regard to the legal requirements of a contract, whether the contract has been breached and any potential remedy the client may have in contract law. Refer to chapter 10 in *Revise SQE: Contract Law*.

EVALUATING YOUR ANSWER

When you have attempted question 2, mark it yourself against the SQE2 legal drafting assessment criteria. Do you think your attempt met the threshold standard?

Now compare your attempt with the following key legal points and two sample answers to question 2. A circled number indicates that commentary is provided for this part of the answer. The commentary explains whether or not the sample satisfies the assessment criteria, and accordingly likely to meet the threshold SQE2 standard.

➡ Key legal points: Question 2

- Ensure that the document complies with CPR 16.5.
- Set out a concise statement of the facts on which the defendant relies and deal with all allegations in a clear and logical manner. Remember that the defence is very important as it sets out the defendant's case and responds to all the allegations in the particulars of claim. Failure to deal with any allegation can have a detrimental effect on the defendant's case.
- Ensure the defence includes:
  - the correct parties to the contract
  - the nature and terms of the contract (referring to any oral or written agreement)
  - oral variations to the contract, giving details
  - performance by the defendant (completion of the works)
  - payment by the claimant
  - disputed breach by the defendant (in accordance with instructions).
- Have regard to CPR 16.5 (1) which says that the defendant must state in the defence which allegations in the particulars of claim they deny, which allegations they are unable to admit or deny but which they require the claimant to prove, and those allegations which are admitted. Remember that CPR 16.5 (2) states that if the defendant denies an allegation, they must state the reason for doing so; and if they intend to put forward a different version of events from that given, they must state their own version.
- If a defendant fails to deal with an allegation but sets out in the defence the nature of the case in relation to the issue, the court will assume that the allegation is to be proven.
- Use instructions to complete the heading and the statement of truth. Ensure that your statement or truth complies with CPR 22 (2.1).

■ SAMPLE ANSWER 1 TO QUESTION 2

Claim No. MC202424A

IN THE WESTBY
COUNTY COURT

BETWEEN

Hanah Ahmed   **Claimant**

and

Flower Club Ltd ❶   **Defendant**

DEFENCE

1. Paragraph 1 of the particulars of claim is admitted. ❷
2. Paragraph 2 of the particulars of claim is admitted.
3. Paragraph 3.1 of the particulars of claim is admitted.
4. As to paragraph 3.2 save that is admitted there was an agreement that the Defendant should arrive at 9 AM on 31 March to install the displays the Defendant avers that due to an unforeseen and unexpected traffic incident on the M6 motorway which halted traffic for 2.5 hours the Defendant arrived at 11.30 AM and completed the floral displays by 6.30 PM and had exited the Claimant's property at 6.45 PM prior to the event starting at 7 PM. ❸
5. As to paragraph 4 of the particulars of claim the Defendant will state as follows:-
   a) The Defendant admits the implied terms pursuant to the Consumer Rights Act 2015 ('the Act') applies to the contract for the supply of the products and the installation thereafter. ❹
   b) The Defendant denies that the quality of the products supplied fell below the standard expected pursuant to Section 9(2) of the Act. Further, the Defendant avers that the products supplied were of good quality and that as natural products the Claimant was warned on delivery that different environments could affect the stability of the product. ❺
6. The Defendant will say that the Claimant's underfloor heating caused the products to dry out and become unstable. The Defendant warned the Claimant of this possibility, requesting that the underfloor heating be paused for the duration of the event but the Claimant refused to do so. ❻
7. Further the Defendant avers that the Claimant was informed via email dated 4 February 202# about the issues with suppliers of dried pampas due to unprecedented weather conditions and that the Defendant gave the Claimant the option of creating three floral clouds of the same size or two large and two smaller clouds, and the Claimant accordingly opted for the latter option. ❼
8. Further and in the alternative the Defendant will say that a guest at the Claimant's event fell against the floral arch causing it to be destroyed and thereafter the Claimant's guests walked over the floral display and in doing so walked the product into the carpet and caused the transfer of dye to the upholstery.
9. The Defendant maintains that the pampas clouds became unstable when party guests opened champagne bottles and sprayed the contents at the displays, causing the wet pampas to become detached and ultimately leading to colour transfer from the wet product onto upholstery. ❽
10. The Defendant denies breach of Section 9(3) under the Act and avers that the products supplied were fit for all the purposes for which goods of that kind are usually supplied, namely
    a) possessed a good appearance and finish;
    b) were free from minor defects;
    c) were safe and durable.

11. The Defendant denies breach of Section 10(3) of the Act that the goods were reasonably fit for purpose and that once completed complied with the Claimant's requirement. The Defendant took several photographs of her work and these are annexed to this defence. **9**

12. The Defendant denies breach of Section 11(1) of the Act and maintains that the goods as described on the Defendant's website matched their description. The Defendant will say that the Claimant made no mention of her dissatisfaction with the products on the day of the event and went as far as to compliment the Defendant's work, taking images and posting them on social media. **10**

13. The Defendant denies breach of Section 49(1) of the Act and avers that the service and installation was carried out with reasonable care and skill. The Defendant completed the installation prior to the event starting and the Claimant complimented the Defendant once the displays were completed, stating that the displays were 'beautiful' and that her guests would be impressed. **11**

14. The Defendant disputes each and every head of loss and damage. The Defendant avers that the cause of the damaged carpet and upholstery was due to the underfloor heating, and the Claimant's guests' subsequent behaviour.

15. It is admitted that the Claimant is entitled to interest. No further admissions can be made in respect of the rate and duration of interest. The Defendant avers that interest is at the discretion of the court and notes that interest on past losses runs at half the special account rate. **12**

STATEMENT OF TRUTH

I believe that the facts stated in this Defence are true. I understand that proceedings for contempt of court may be brought against anyone who makes, or causes to be made, a false statement in a document verified by a statement of truth without an honest belief in its truth.

Full name: Emily Jenkins

Director of Flower Club Ltd **13**

Name of Defendant's legal representative's firm: Conifer LLP

Signature *Conifer LLP*

Date: 23 June 202#

Documents in these proceedings may be served on the Defendant at the following address: Conifer LLP, 1 High Street, Lytham St Annes, Lancashire FY8 1DA

COMMENTARY

1 The correct names of the parties are stated in the defence. The name of the action will follow the names as stated in the particulars of claim, so the candidate needs to make sure that they copy the correct court header from the particulars of claim.

2 Remember when drafting a defence that the document must comply with CPR 16.5(1), which states that the defence must deal with every allegation raised in the particulars of claim, stating which allegations are denied, which allegations are admitted, and which allegations the defendant is unable to admit or deny, but requires the claimant to prove (sometimes referred to as a 'non-admission'). Failure to deny an allegation will result in that allegation being admitted (CPR 16.5(5)) and the defendant being unable to revisit the allegation should the matter proceed to trial. Here the candidate has mirrored the numbering of the particulars of claim, adhering to the necessity to structure the document appropriately and logically as per the SQE2 assessment criteria.

3 It is important to specify why particular allegations are denied or an alternative argument presented. In this paragraph, the candidate is providing the court with the timings of the completion of the installation, to prove that the defendant did not breach this section of the Act.

4 This paragraph is admitted as the Consumer Rights Act 2015 applies to the supply of the goods and the services provided by the defendant in this scenario. The purpose of the defence is to define and narrow the issues between the parties, and it would be unreasonable and incorrect to deny the application of the Consumer Rights Act 2015. Here the candidate is ensuring that the document is legally effective and also narrowing the issues for the court to deal with at an eventual trial.

5 Remember that complying with CPR 1.1 and 1.3 requires the parties to assist the court and ensure that all information is provided so that the court has the relevant details with which to deal with the claim. In this paragraph and the next, the candidate denies the allegations, and provides alternative argument in this respect.

6 The defendant gives an alternative argument in respect of the allegation in compliance with CPR 16.5.

7 This paragraph provides more information regarding the counter-argument in respect of the allegations in the previous paragraph.

8 These paragraphs provide further specific details and more information pursuant to the client's instructions and information provided. Here the candidate is ensuring that the document is drafted with client focus as per the SQE2 assessment criteria.

9 Documents can be annexed to any statement of case or defence, and once disclosure is dealt with, these documents will provide further insight into the evidence. However, at this stage it is reasonable to
attach the images that the client downloaded from the claimant's social media platforms in order to provide some context to the denials in the defence.

10 Again here the candidate is complying with CPR 1.1 and 1.3 in providing specific information in respect of the allegations. These documents will form part of the defendant's disclosure in due course.

11 Including quotes in the defence is acceptable and illustrates that the information provided by the client is being used to compile the defence. The client will go into further detail about this point in her witness statement, but highlighting it now in the defence sets the scene for the client's own oral evidence.

12 It is common for claimant solicitors to plead interest at 8%, but case law in respect of interest on past losses states that interest runs at half the special account rate. The candidate is therefore correct to concede that the claimant is entitled to some interest but to state that interest is at the discretion of the court (as this is always the case) and assert the counter-argument in respect of the rate of interest.

13 Here the defendant signs the statement of truth in the defence, and does so as director of a limited company. Here the candidate is complying with the SQE assessment criteria in ensuring that the document is verified by a statement of truth and complies with CPR 22(2.1).

Does this answer meet the threshold?

The sample answer contains all of the information that the client requires and that the candidate has been asked to provide. The candidate has adhered to the SQE2 assessment criteria in that they have used clear, precise, concise and acceptable language. The candidate has structured the document logically and dealt with each allegation as per CPR 16.5. The answer is therefore likely to meet the threshold standard for SQE2 legal writing.

Now consider the second sample answer to question 2.

SAMPLE ANSWER 2 TO QUESTION 2

Claim No. MC202424A

IN THE WESTBY
COUNTY COURT

BETWEEN

Hanah Ahmed   **Claimant**

and

Emily Jenkin ❶   **Defendant**

DEFENCE

1. The Defendant is the director of a floral supplier and installation company and was commissioned to create some pampas clouds and floral arch for the Claimant's party on 31 March. ❷
2. The Defendant will say that she arrived late at the Claimant's house due to traffic issues.
3. The Defendant denies breach of duty under the Consumer Rights Act.
4. The Claimant asked the Defendant to complete two large pampas clouds and two small pampas clouds and that is what the Defendant did. ❸
5. The Claimant avers that the products supplied were of good quality. ❹
6. Any issues with the product was the fault of the Claimant in that she insisted on having underfloor heating turned on and her guests were badly behaved and awfully drunk. They sprayed champagne into the pampas clouds, making them disintegrate. ❺
7. The Defendant will say that the goods matched the website and that they were safe and durable, also that the Defendant installed them with skill. ❻
8. The Defendant will not reimburse the Claimant and disputes the cost of the damaged carpets and upholstery. ❼
9. The Defendant denies the claim for interest.
10. Statement of truth. ❽

I believe that the facts stated in this defence are true. I understand that proceedings for contempt of court may be brought against anyone who makes, or causes to be made, a false statement in a document verified by a statement of truth without an honest belief in its truth.

Full name: Emily Jenkins

Name of Defendant's legal representative's firm: Conifer LLP

Signature: *Conifer LLP*

Date: 23 June 202#

Documents in these proceedings may be served on the Defendant at the following address: Conifer LLP, 1 High Street, Lytham St Annes, Lancashire FY8 1DA

COMMENTARY

1 The parties' names have not been copied identically on the court header from the particulars of claim. It is important to reiterate the court header as the parties' names will provide the name of the case throughout the action. In order to meet the SQE2 assessment criteria, the candidate must draft a document that is legally correct.

2 This paragraph in itself is not incorrect, but when drafting a defence it is advisable to deal with each paragraph of the particulars of claim methodically to provide a response. Remember that parties are under an obligation to narrow the issues and to provide clear and concise information in order for the court to deal with the claim. The SQE2 assessment criteria requires candidates to use clear, precise and acceptable language.

3 Pursuant to CPR 16.5(2) where an allegation is denied, reasons for this denial must be given, and it should be stated if the defendant intends to put forward a different version of events. It is not sufficient to plead a denial, even though the candidate then sets out facts which if proved could provide a complete defence to the claim. Failure to comply with CPR 16.5(2) is contrary to the SQE2 assessment criteria to draft documents which are legally comprehensive and correct.

4 Further to point 3 above, the candidate must deny the allegation and then set out their version of events or counter-argument.

5 The candidate has not provided enough detail here. The client has provided sufficient information which can be specifically referred to in the defence, to support the defendant's denial of each allegation contained in the particulars of a claim. According to the assessment criteria, the candidate needs to exercise judgement and ensure that the client's instructions are followed in sufficient detail.

6 The claimant has pleaded specific allegations of breach under sections 9, 10, 11 and 49 of the Consumer Rights Act 2015, therefore it is appropriate to deal with each allegation in turn and state which section of the Act the defendant is denying breaching. This paragraph is vague and does not address each section of the Act as the particulars of claim set out, nor does it specify which allegations the defendant is denying. Contrary to the SQE2 assessment criteria, the document is not legally correct as the candidate has failed to deal with each allegation.

7 Pursuant to CPR 16.5(2) where an allegation is denied – whether it be in respect of liability or quantum (value) – reasons for this denial must be given. The candidate is required to specifically deal with each head of loss and state whether it is admitted, denied or put the claimant to strict proof of the existence of that head of loss. Here a blanket denial of special damages is too general. If the SQE2 assessment asked you to draft a document with a separate schedule of special damages, then you would need to draft a separate document to accompany the defence. The claimant served a separate schedule of special damages attached to the particulars of claim, the defendant could also serve a separate counter schedule of special damages annexed to the defence.

8 The statement of truth should not be a numbered paragraph – it should be set out separately in compliance with the template provided. It is also appropriate to mention that Emily Jenkins is the director of the limited company against which the cause of action has been brought. Failure to correctly complete the statement of truth can render the document not legally correct, contrary to the SQE2 assessment criteria.

Does this answer meet the threshold?

When assessing the second defence against the SQE2 legal drafting assessment criteria, it is unlikely that this defence would meet the threshold standard for SQE2 legal drafting. The answer falls short as it does not deal with every allegation in a logical manner and at times does not use precise, concise or acceptable language. The defence represents the defendant's response to the claimant's allegations and must be legally comprehensive.

■ KEY POINT CHECKLIST

This chapter has covered the following key knowledge points:
- The SQE2 assessment criteria for legal drafting and how to apply them in the context of dispute resolution in contract and tort.
- A suggested structure for approaching an SQE2 legal drafting question.
- Examples of pleadings which might or might not meet the threshold standard, with full commentary on their strengths and weaknesses.

■ SUMMARY AND REFLECTION

To give yourself the best chance of success in the SQE2 legal drafting assessment, take your time to read the question properly and consider the legal points the question is asking of you. Draw up a short plan to structure your pleadings.

One element of the assessment criteria is to use 'clear, precise, concise and acceptable' language. You need to bear in mind whilst drafting that you are creating a document for the court and other parties, so you need to show the examiner that you can write clearly and accurately.

As well as understanding the relevant fundamental legal principles, you will need to apply them correctly to the facts of the client's case, whether it be a breach of contract or negligence claim as contained in this chapter. Remember to consider the facts, the relevant issues and how the law applies to the resolution of the dispute from the point of view of the client.

Ensure that you draft the document in compliance with the CPR. The type of claim can dictate what documents you need to annex or plead in the particulars or defence. You also need to understand how to complete the statement of truth, so practise drafting the correct wording.

Now take the time to reflect and consider what you might still need to work on, and whether you feel completely confident in your legal writing skills in the context of dispute resolution.

Final words

We hope that the guidance and examples contained in this book have helped to put into context how to use your practice skills to ensure you reach the SQE2 grading criteria. Remember, above all, this is an assessment and the examiner needs to see evidence that you have met the criteria in order for you to pass the threshold. Always keep this in the back of your mind when taking your SQE2 assessments.

While this book is designed to aid your learning and provide helpful tips on how to pass your SQE2 assessments, it is no substitute for practice. All skills are improved with repetition and refining your technique, and legal skills are no exception to this rule. Take any opportunity you can to write letters, draft legal documents, and practise your interviewing and advocacy skills. Reflect carefully on your performance after each exercise:
• What could you have done better?
• Did you meet all of the grading criteria applicable to that particular skill?
• Do you need to fill any gaps in your legal knowledge?

Constant practice and self-reflection are the keys to success.

Finally, the team at *Revise SQE* wish you the best of luck in your SQE2 assessments!

Appendix

PERFORMANCE INDICATORS FOR SQE2
CASE AND MATTER ANALYSIS ASSESSMENT CRITERIA

Skills	Indicators demonstrating competence	Indicators that do not demonstrate competence
Identify relevant facts	• The candidate selects facts that are important in ensuring the client's needs/objectives are met, or are relevant to the legal analysis, from the documentation provided	• The candidate refers to all facts from the documentation, regardless of whether or not they are important in meeting the client's objectives or relevant to their legal analysis • The candidate refers only to irrelevant facts • The candidate does not refer to sufficient relevant facts to support the legal analysis
Provide client-focused advice (ie advice that demonstrates an understanding of the problem from the client's point of view and what the client wants to achieve, not just from a legal perspective)	• The candidate demonstrates an understanding of the client's problem from the client's perspective • The candidate addresses the client's legal problem, any relevant commercial considerations and/or the client's personal circumstances, priorities, objectives and constraints	• The candidate does not approach or appreciate the client's problem from the client's perspective • The candidate does not focus on the issues identified by the client
Use clear, precise, concise and acceptable language	• The reader understands the candidate's use of language and clarity of expression • The candidate avoids unnecessary technical terms/legal jargon	• The reader struggles to understand the candidate's use of language; the answer lacks clarity and/or is poorly expressed • The reader's understanding is adversely affected by the density, length or brevity of the answer • The candidate uses unnecessary technical terms/legal jargon

Law	Indicators demonstrating competence	Indicators that do not demonstrate competence
Apply the law correctly to the client's situation	• The candidate identifies the relevant fundamental legal principles in accordance with the SQE2 assessment specification and applies them correctly to the facts of the client's case	• The candidate does not identify and correctly apply the relevant legal principles to the facts of the client's case • The candidate does not apply the relevant legal principles in a way that addresses the client's needs and concerns
Apply the law comprehensively to the client's situation, identifying any ethical and professional conduct issues and exercising judgement to resolve them honestly and with integrity	• The candidate's legal analysis is sufficiently detailed in the context of the client's case, eg assessing information to identify key issues and risks; reaching reasonable conclusions supported by relevant evidence • Where relevant, the candidate recognises ethical issues and exercises effective judgement in addressing them in accordance with the SRA Principles and rules of professional conduct	• The candidate's legal analysis is not sufficiently detailed in the context of the client's case, eg the candidate demonstrates little or no understanding of the key issues and risks; fails to apply the law to the facts to reach reasonable conclusions • The candidate does not recognise ethical issues or exercise effective judgement in addressing them in accordance with the SRA Principles and rules of professional conduct

PERFORMANCE INDICATORS FOR SQE2
LEGAL RESEARCH ASSESSMENT CRITERIA

Skills	Indicators demonstrating competence	Indicators that do not demonstrate competence
Identify and use relevant sources and information	• The candidate selects relevant information about the legal issue, or the client's problem, from the primary and/or secondary sources provided, eg o the candidate identifies relevant legislation/cases and/or legal explanations/ commentary in a practitioner's text, or legal encyclopaedia o the candidate extracts relevant material, such as particular provision(s) from a statute, or legal rule(s) from the Civil Procedure Rules • The candidate uses their findings to substantiate/ support their answer to the question(s) asked	• The candidate selects only irrelevant information from the primary and/or secondary sources provided • The candidate selects insufficient relevant information from the primary and/or secondary sources provided • The candidate is unable to distinguish between information that is relevant to the legal issue or the client's problem, and information that is irrelevant, eg the candidate's answer contains information drawn from all sources regardless of relevance, or from a number of irrelevant sources • The candidate does not use their findings to substantiate/ support the answer to the question(s) asked
Provide advice that is client-focused and addresses the client's problem	• The candidate demonstrates an understanding of the client's problem from the client's perspective, eg the candidate addresses the client's legal problem, any relevant commercial considerations and/or the client's priorities, objectives and constraints	• The candidate does not understand the problem from the client's perspective, eg they focus on irrelevant issues/provide advice that does not take into account the client's priorities, objectives or constraints, or is inappropriate for the client's situation
Use clear, precise, concise and acceptable language	• The candidate uses understandable and simple language to convey facts and information effectively • The candidate uses correct legal terminology where necessary	• The reader struggles to understand the candidate's use of language; the answer lacks clarity and/or is poorly expressed • The reader's understanding is adversely affected by the density or brevity of the answer • The candidate uses unnecessary or confusing technical terms/legal jargon

Law	Indicators demonstrating competence	Indicators that do not demonstrate competence
Apply the law correctly to the client's situation	• The candidate identifies the relevant legal principles and applies them correctly to the facts of the client's case	• The candidate does not identify and apply the correct legal principles to the facts of the client's case • The candidate identifies the correct legal principles but misapplies them to the client's case
Apply the law comprehensively to the client's situation, identifying any ethical and professional conduct issues and exercising judgement to resolve them honestly and with integrity	• The candidate's legal analysis is sufficiently detailed in the context of the facts of the case, eg the candidate draws on multiple sources of information to address the legal issue/client's problem effectively • Where relevant, the candidate recognises ethical issues and exercises effective judgement in addressing them in accordance with the SRA Principles and rules of professional conduct	• The candidate's legal analysis is not sufficiently detailed in the context of the facts of the client's case • The candidate does not recognise ethical issues or exercise effective judgement in addressing them in accordance with the SRA Principles and rules of professional conduct

PERFORMANCE INDICATORS FOR SQE2 LEGAL WRITING ASSESSMENT CRITERIA

Skills	Indicators demonstrating competence	Indicators that do not demonstrate competence
Include relevant facts	• The candidate refers to and/ or addresses the salient facts provided in their instructions. Salient facts could include facts that are important in ensuring the client's needs/objectives are met, or relevant to legal advice	• The candidate includes many facts in their answer that have no bearing on their legal advice
Use a logical structure	• The candidate's presentation of information is well organised, set out clearly and easy to follow • The reader is able to understand the candidate's answer without difficulty	• The candidate's presentation of information is confused and rambling • The reader is unable to follow or understand the candidate's answer
Advice/content is client- and recipient-focused	• The candidate demonstrates an understanding of the client's circumstances including their needs, objectives and priorities • The candidate, where relevant and appropriate, explores options and advises on strategies and solutions • The candidate takes into account who the client is; recognises the key issues in the case and considers any risks • Where appropriate, the candidate imparts any difficult or unwelcome news clearly and sensitively	• The candidate does not understand the client's perspective, eg they focus on irrelevant issues/provide extraneous advice/fail to advise on relevant options, strategies and solutions • The candidate fails to take into account who the client is and does not recognise the key issues in the case or consider any risks • The candidate lacks empathy or sensitivity if imparting difficult or unwelcome news
Use clear, precise, concise and acceptable language that is appropriate to the recipient	• The reader understands the candidate's use of language and clarity of expression • The candidate's language is appropriate to the recipient and the situation • The candidate avoids unnecessary technical terms/ legal jargon • The candidate uses formalities appropriate to the context and purpose of the communication	• The reader struggles to understand the candidate's use of language; the answer lacks clarity and/or is poorly expressed • The reader's understanding is adversely affected by the density or brevity of the answer • The candidate uses language that is not appropriate to the recipient and/or the situation, eg the candidate adopts an essay-style approach • The candidate uses unnecessary or confusing technical terms/legal jargon

Law	Indicators demonstrating competence	Indicators that do not demonstrate competence
Apply the law correctly to the client's situation	• The candidate identifies the correct legal principles and applies them correctly to the facts of the case	• The candidate does not identify the correct legal principles • The candidate does not apply the legal principles correctly to the client's situation
Apply the law comprehensively to the client's situation, identifying any ethical and professional conduct issues and exercising judgement to resolve them honestly and with integrity	• The candidate's writing is of sufficient detail in the context of the client's situation and the relevant factual and legal issues • Where relevant, the candidate recognises ethical issues and exercises effective judgement in addressing them in accordance with the SRA Principles and rules of professional conduct	• The candidate's writing is not sufficiently detailed in the context of the client's situation and the relevant factual and legal issues • The candidate does not recognise ethical issues or exercise effective judgement in addressing them in accordance with the SRA Principles and rules of professional conduct

PERFORMANCE INDICATORS FOR SQE2 LEGAL DRAFTING ASSESSMENT CRITERIA

Skills	Indicators demonstrating competence	Indicators that do not demonstrate competence
Use clear, precise, concise and acceptable language	• The candidate uses understandable and simple language to convey facts and information effectively • The candidate uses words and phrases that are suitably formal for the document being drafted • The candidate uses correct legal terminology where necessary • The document uses as few words as possible without compromising the quality of the answer	• The candidate's answer is consistently wordy, repetitive or confusing and cannot be easily understood • The meaning of the document cannot be ascertained because it contains few words • The candidate uses inappropriate language, eg the language is too informal or casual • The candidate uses unnecessary technical terms/ legal jargon throughout
Structure the document appropriately and logically	• The candidate presents facts and information in a methodical way, eg the focus, flow and direction of each paragraph is clear and appropriate signposts are used to guide the reader through the document • The way in which the candidate sets out the contents of the document achieve its purpose	• The candidate's arrangement of facts or information is disjointed or confusing, eg the paragraphing or sequencing of information is illogical • The way in which the candidate sets out the contents of the document does not achieve its purpose
Law	Indicators demonstrating competence	Indicators that do not demonstrate competence
Draft a document that is legally correct	• The candidate identifies the correct legal principles in accordance with the SQE2 assessment specification and applies them correctly in their drafting • The candidate's drafting is legally effective, eg the document contains all key information or the names of relevant parties	• The candidate does not identify the correct legal principles • The candidate does not apply the legal principles correctly in their drafting • The candidate's drafting is not legally effective
Draft a document that is legally comprehensive, identifying any ethical and professional conduct issues and exercising judgement to resolve them honestly and with integrity	• The candidate's drafting is sufficiently detailed in the context of the client's situation and the relevant factual and legal issues • Where relevant, the candidate recognises ethical issues and exercises effective judgement in addressing them in accordance with the SRA Principles and rules of professional conduct	• The candidate's drafting is not sufficiently detailed in the context of the client's situation and the relevant factual and legal issues • The candidate does not recognise ethical issues or exercise effective judgement in addressing them in accordance with the SRA Principles and rules of professional conduct